# DIGESTED BY THE DUST

# DIGESTED
## by the
# DUST

**STARK HUNTER**

Book Design & Production
Columbus Publishing Lab
www.ColumbusPublishingLab.com

Copyright 2018 by Stark Hunter
LCCN 2018947918

Published By Mind Tavern Books

Artwork credit for Mind Tavern Books logo: Stephanie Moore

All rights reserved. No part of this book may be reproduced or transmitted in any form or by any means, electronic or mechanical, including photocopying, recording, or by any information storage and retrieval system, without permission in writing from the copyright owner.

Paperback ISBN: 978-1-63337-208-5
E-book ISBN: 978-1-63337-209-2

The "Prologue" and "Epilogue" are excerpts from the novel, In A Gadda Da Vida, by Stark Hunter, copyright 2001.

Photo of Mt. Olive Cemetery (page 5), courtesy of the Whittier Public Library.

This book was printed in the United States of America.

1 3 5 7 9 10 8 6 4 2

# CONTENTS

| | |
|---|---|
| Introduction | i |
| Prologue: "The Poet's Remembrances of Clark Cemetery in 1963" | 1 |
| Part One: The Voices From Clark Cemetery (73 epitaphs) | 5 |
| A Photographic Haunting in Mt. Olive Cemetery (circa 1935) | 145 |
| Part Two: The Voices From Mt. Olive Cemetery (77 epitaphs) | 145 |
| Epilogue: "The Poet's Remembrances of His First Visit to Mt. Olive Cemetery- May, 1964" | 289 |

*This anthology of epitaphs is respectfully dedicated to the hearty pioneers mentioned in this book, who lived and died in Whittier, California, and are now buried in Founders Park, once known as Clark and Mt. Olive Cemeteries.*

"To this generation I would say:
Memorize some bit of verse of truth or beauty.
It may serve a turn in your life…"

"Mrs. George Reece"
Spoon River Anthology
Edgar Lee Masters
1915

# INTRODUCTION

Sixteen miles east of Los Angeles lies the quiet quaint town of Whittier. Settled in 1887 by Midwest Quakers in search of a suitable home for their religious colony, the town was a veritable utopia at first with its mild, ideal weather conditions and its thousands of acres of rich, fertile soil for growing a wide variety of flowers, fruits and vegetables, not to mention the myriad variety of trees that would eventually bring a merciful shade in summer to the many homes that took root in the late 19th Century.

Named after Quaker poet, John Greenleaf Whittier, the town enjoyed immense growth in its formative years, especially when the Southern Pacific Railroad brought relatives and visitors to its sun-drenched locale.

But shortly after Whittier's founding, a diphtheria epidemic took the lives of several citizens. Not having a cemetery in which to bury these departed souls, Willit Dorland, one of the town's early arrivals, donated two acres of his ranch land for Whittier's first cemetery. And for ten years he cared for the cemetery grounds with the help of his family. When Dorland passed away at the turn of the century, his daughter, Artilissa Dorland Clark, took over the chores of caring for the cemetery, and this she did with fervent devotion until the 1930's when old age and ill health precluded this on-going upkeep. After Artilissa's death in 1940, the cemetery became an eyesore. The city of Whittier, after all, did not own this private property and virtually did nothing to stop the proliferation of weeds and the wanton acts of vandalism to the tombstones.

Sometime in the late 50's (the last burial was in 1958 on the west side), the city erected a barbed wire fence around the grounds and posted "No Trespassing" signs on the gates. As a child growing up in late 50's Whittier, I well recall this old, run-down graveyard, and inexplicably, developed a life-long fascination for this meager tract of forbidden landscape. And it all began in 1963 when I was eleven years old.

This culminating anthology includes 150 epitaphs, extracted from two preceding volumes: *Voices From Clark Cemetery*, and its sequel, *Voices From Mt. Olive Cemetery*. Mention must be made here that the names of "The Voices" are real, and their life dates are accurate as well, based on official burial lists obtained from the Whittier Public library. Each deceased person speaks from their grave in extended epitaph form, revealing their life's highlights, personal insights on existence, statements of faith, tragedies, sicknesses, heartbreaks, long-held secrets, victories and defeats, and most of them reveal how they died and how they feel about being dead. Moreover, the speakers randomly chosen for inclusion in these pages actually lived and died in Whittier during the turn of the 20th Century. Some of their stories are true, based on research done by Paul Moore, a retired history teacher from Whittier. Most others, though, because of a lack of information available, are my own "educated" inferences of the truth about each person, and then filtered by my own poetic imagination. Mention should be made here, that all the descriptions of Whittier's streets, important buildings, parks, and it's other unique geographical landmarks, contained therein, are accurate and authentic. The setting for this final volume when seen as a whole, is more than a collection of poems, but also, it is a unified poetic drama with several connecting subtexts. The dead people whose names appear in this work are my actors and actresses so to speak, and they have all been assigned their roles in telling the stories contained therein; the words they recite are their dialogue, as written by me, their living playwright.

As with Edgar Lee Masters' book, Spoon River Anthology, I did not

## INTRODUCTION

seek permission from the dead to use their names in this book, and I did not seek permission from any of their living ancestors. If any of the dead object to the stories assigned to them, I apologize, and will take it up with that person after I die. As for the living who object, well, I apologize again. Please sue me! I would love the buzz! But most courts of law won't rule against writers for "defaming" a dead person, especially a person who has been deceased for over a hundred years. Nevertheless, I am sure they (the voices) are all quite amused (in spirit) by the attention and remembrances of their long-ago, forgotten lives, as portrayed in this poetry volume.

One final note to the reader: Usually epitaphs are short pieces with succinct language, found on a dead person's tombstone, summing up that person's life in a witty, unique way. But mine, obviously, are in extended form, allowing for more narrative elements to be included, thus giving the entire work an interesting literary cohesion. Roscoe Settle, who died at age 23 in 1906, is the central and most interesting "voice" in this anthology. I advise the reader to read the epitaphs from Poem 1 to Poem 150 without skipping or veering off course. I hope you enjoy this poetic journey to the Other Side.

Stark Hunter<br>
May, 2018

# PROLOGUE

## THE POET'S REMEMBRANCES OF CLARK CEMETERY IN 1963

This neglected, rather eerie looking place gave me the creeps whenever I walked by as an eleven year old boy in 1963. An ivy-covered, barbed wire fence surrounded this run-down necropolis on all four sides, and it was divided into halves of one acre each by Citrus Road which ran north up to Beverly Boulevard. The interior of Clark Cemetery could only be seen through its two rusted gates which were located adjacent to each other on Broadway and Citrus Streets. On each unobstructed gate was a conspicuous "No Trespassing" sign, placed there by the Whittier Police Department, promising a hefty fine if caught inside.

As I slowly made my way to Hoover Street on all those warm late summer afternoons, I would invariably stop at the Broadway gate and peer through the metal links, and there inside that almost surreal tract of forgotten land, were row upon row of old tombstones with large, distinctly carved surnames of the deceased prominently displayed on the facades. In front of me on a mound of dry hard earth was the large broad tombstone with the imposing name of "Hadley," and as I stood there in the afternoon sun and smog, I remember studying the corroded deteriorating condition of the monument, eaten away by many years of rain and wind and sun, and I recall wondering what kind of life this man named "Hadley" led while alive back in the early days of the century and how he died.

From my vantage point on the outside of that old weather-beaten gate, I remember squinting my eyes to see the death date of "1905," and strangely, I would stand there transfixed as if indelibly glued to the street and stare for sometimes up to twenty minutes at the big, almost scary name "Hadley," and then my eyes would wander to the other stone monuments, many of which were toppled over and laying desolate beside their horizontal pedestals. And the place was completely overrun with deep dense weeds and bits of strewn garbage that had been blown over the barbed wire by strong Santa Ana Winds from the east, and there was a multiplicity of decomposing leaves and desiccated twigs from the antique walnut trees and desert palms that blanketed this bleak, hollowed ground.

Facing north from this padlocked gate, I remember being irresistibly drawn in by two rows of tall desert palm trees that spanned the entire width of the eastern half of Clark Cemetery. With eleven trees on each side, it was evident that these tall "guardians of the dead" were planted nearly a hundred years before to form a central avenue by which a funeral procession could enter into the cemetery, and then after the hearse had safely entered inside, there were three convergent rows facing east and west that led even further into the central interior. Now in an obvious state of desuetude, this shadowy avenue leading from the outside gate was but a dirty dusty road in 1963 with protruding rocks and moribund weeds, and time now had transformed this "avenue into eternity" into something sad and cursed, like death. To my way of thinking, it was as if Clark Cemetery itself had died a long time ago and now it too desperately needed a proper, dignified burial. I truly felt bad for the dead inside and couldn't understand why this quiet final resting place, a place that should be held sacred by the town, had become the decayed mess that it was.

After spending quite a few minutes staring through the eastern gate, I slowly crossed Citrus Road and spent the same amount of time shaking my head and looking through the faded metal links of the gate which led into the western half of the cemetery. This side was even more dense and dark and depressing than the eastern half, for on this side, the walnut trees, now fully mature and overgrown, had been planted very close together so very long ago, and the brownish green weeds were completely obscuring the ground and all of the hundreds of gasping tombstones. It was like staring into the deep mouth of death itself, and the barbed wire fence and locked gate now prevented me from entering inside to be swallowed whole into its black consuming belly. The only tombstone that I could partially see from the western gate was located directly in front of me, a little to the right with the name "Hunnicutt" prominently carved between laurel leaves and the Gates of Heaven.

I recall finding this western gate on Citrus Road to be quite fascinating for it was upheld by two identical slabs of compressed concrete, rising at least ten feet, and out of each slab there was a skinny vertical plumber's pipe which formed an empty hollow frame of two horizontal pipes, and each extended at least fifteen feet over to the other vertical pipe on the right, and when one stood and stared at this portal, it appeared that this frame used to be a former sign which probably said "Mount Olive Cemetery," and in my mind I remember envisioning a funeral procession back in the 1890's entering the cemetery under that sign with all the survivors wearing plaintive black raiment, and if one could somehow measure all the tears that had been shed within this place down through the decades, it probably would quench the thirst of all those walnut and palm trees that now silently groaned in front of me for attention and live human contact.

Many times during the ensuing weeks and months, I made my solemn afternoon visits to the two gates of the forgotten and condemned Clark Cemetery, and with each visit I developed a strong obsessive longing to actually step inside and walk among the angry tombstones to simply assuage their loneliness and bitterness. Since the cemetery was permanently locked up, I truly felt this would never happen. With the passage of inexorable time, I was proved wrong.

## PART ONE

# THE VOICES FROM CLARK CEMETERY

# THE VOICES FROM CLARK CEMETERY

POEM 1

# SUDIE NELSON
# 1875–1906

I saw ten thousand western sunsets,

And sang Happy Birthday to my father

In the old parlor room there on Hadley Street

Until 1902. And I wept there,

Amongst the throw-rugs and potted ferns,

On many a vexing occasion,

Over the blue eyes, and charming repartee

Of Roscoe Settle.

I gave him my heart, although much younger,

And he settled all those dandelion doubts I had,

Concerning my age and inherent pulchritude,

By giving me his one last "cheerio,"

And disappearing from town in 1904.

It seems all so silly and trivial now,

Those nagging mundane details

Of one huge human heartbreak.

In the winter of '05 I caught cold.

But the fireplace could not repair my despair.

I'm fine now, "settled" in this dust.

At last with him forever!

DIGESTED BY THE DUST

POEM 2

# MILTON SANDERS
# 1846–1891

There were days when I wished I could die,

And numbing nights when I shuddered in a feverish night sweat,

Fearing that I would not live.

Oh to have those precious delightful days back again!

I could climb my mountain once more,

And exult in the caresses of unstoppable time.

I lived my pensive days by the new hotel in town.

And took long walks down an avenue of fiery pepper trees.

It was on Washington Avenue I met Ruhama.

She was but a girl when I took her hand into mine.

My soul and hers embraced like clouds in the night,

When doors and windows are closed

And only little glimpses of strange light appear.

We lived through decades of summers and winters,

Rainstorms and heat waves,

Weddings and days of grief.

And how could I ever forget

The early morning coffee times in the kitchen before work.

Ten thousand glorious times we awoke together

Inside the curtained, perfumed sanctuary of Ruhama,

The solitary love of my life!

Weep not for my grave here.

# THE VOICES FROM CLARK CEMETERY

Please don't weep or shed a tear.

I died happy at 45,

And the folks put me here in Clark Cemetery.

But it is good here.

I can enjoy the quiet and the scurrying rats

Above my bed at midnight.

DIGESTED BY THE DUST

POEM 3
# ELLA HYDE
# 1857–1898

That cad with the freckle on his forehead,

That rascal man beast,

Handsome as a Greek

But devastatingly insecure,

And so deliciously young!

He was the one who stole my pride,

There, behind the Hadley tombstone in the moonlight,

And who,

Breathlessly and with trembling hands,

Unlatched the ruby red necklace

From around my naked neck that night.

It was he.

That cad who swooped down upon my innocence,

Like a maniacal Zeus

In one of his crazy costumes of concupiscence,

And carried me off to nights of brazen episodes,

Splendid spectacles in light and magic,

Of him and me embracing wildly, madly,

In dreamy dances with caresses and kisses.

Only the truly passionate

Could understand these mad scenes in the dark!

I met RS on many a night

In the long concealing shadows of Central Park.

He was my man, but he didn't know it.

I lived my life here in this dusty town the best I could.

I believe I left my mark in some small but universal way.

At least I knew when to say no to Roscoe Settle.

Now I'd like to go back to my grave and sleep.

I am tired of this rant about The Man Beast.

At 41 I entered here after my bout with diphtheria.

The trees here are my shadowy friends now.

But I sometimes secretly wish I could meet RS.

Just as it was in 1897,

He and I kissing in the garden Gazebo at Central Park,

His hand on the small of my back.

Me trembling with monstrous want,

My ultimate Prince.

Who lied to me like a rat!

# DIGESTED BY THE DUST

POEM 4
# LOUIS RASH
# 1841–1905

I lived in the big white house

On the corner of Painter and La Cuarta.

The people in Quaker town called me Pops

And I worked many a grueling day,

And on many a grueling job,

Through the ebb and flow of distant days,

Both rainy and sunny,

Paving the first roads in town,

Harvesting the citrus crop in season time

And planting a thousand trees with a bronze pickaxe.

I did okay for a farm boy from Illinois.

Life was good

And I was able to feed and clothe my children.

I died that afternoon in April,

In my sixty-fourth year,

As the winds from the east kicked up dust,

And a multitude of memories.

My wife, though, took it hard.

Mr. White brought me here in '05

In his horse-drawn hearse, garlanded in black,

A stiff dead man in a simple wooden coffin made of Pine.

They sang Blessed Be The Tie That Binds

## THE VOICES FROM CLARK CEMETERY

And Pastor Swain said I was a good man.

And I will never forget the swishing of the dirt upon my person,

As Mr. White buried me in my simple grave.

POEM 5

# ETHEL WOODSTOCK
# 1892–1908

Mother, I love you.

Mother I am so sorry I died that night in your arms.

It was a Saturday night at half past 10

And you cried as I died.

Mother, you were my best friend

And we shared all those secrets about him.

And we laughed when we both realized

It was just a silly misunderstanding.

It was all about me, after all.

A young naïve girl just growing up

But never finding out.

Never finding out about the secret conspiracies

Of a boy's selfish soul.

But now I have a confession mommy.

I never told you this, but

I met him in this cemetery one night

In the autumn of '07,

And by the tombstone of Mr. Hadley

He took me behind the full moon shadows of that massive stone,

And I melted there like ice.

Forgive me mother.

Forgive your dead shrunken daughter

## THE VOICES FROM CLARK CEMETERY

Here in this deep darkened grave

Who, after all, didn't know any better.

I miss life.

I miss being young and in love.

I miss my mother and my papa

And I miss my kitty with the orange tail.

And most of all,

I miss the bloom of the jacarandas in June.

DIGESTED BY THE DUST

POEM 6

# FRED SEEGMILLER
# 1871–1907

You never met a man who loved my town.

As I much as I did.

Coming here in '90 by the train.

It nearly killed me, but I stayed on my knees.

I prayed and prayed I would not go mad.

For 15 years I played the organ.

In the magnificent church on Bailey Street.

I played the passions of Bach and the soothings of Handal.

And I served refreshments in the churchyard.

One night in Mid March

After services had concluded,

Rebecca walked into my life.

She coyly received my flirtatious wink

And a family of five was the magical result.

For twelve years I moved lumber by horse and reigns,

And drove the wagonload to the flowering homesteads.

I worked hard, prayed to God

And never forgot to kiss my wife goodbye.

I lived on the end of Olive Street.

Hidden by tall Elms,

Inside my house with the white shutters,

I brought two of my brood into this world

And I watched one leave it in the winter of '99.

It was in that same room,

The one in the back by the myrtle tree,

That I too tasted death.

I had the cancer

And it was eating me like a cannibal unconverted.

And now I am dead and buried in Clark Cemetery.

And my living soul longs to spend just one more minute.

Just one more minute

As a dying man.

My soul is not dead.

My soul is not sad.

Let me sleep now.

POEM 7
# LUELLA BUFKIN
# 1872–1891

Do you remember me?

Does anyone remember the Bufkin girl of Comstock Street?

I was the girl who read her Bible every Sunday

In the forgiving shade of my father's Elm Tree..

Maybe not.

Because I died young… way too young.

And I was a smart pretty girl too.

No one ever knew I spent many waking moments alone.

Alone and staring into the parlor room mirror

Staring into my own blue eyes;

Imagining they were the eyes of my galloping Knight.

Eyes I had hoped to use

In capturing the "devil" by his tail.

I knew how to cook and sew

And clean house and milk the cow.

I made the butter and the bread

And my mother always said

"Now Luella, don't forget to add the yeast."

I cleaned and scrubbed and scoured

And even cut the firewood on occasion.

It was all I knew;

My life with rags and strong soaps;

# THE VOICES FROM CLARK CEMETERY

One continuing, unending back-breaking episode

Of hardwood chores

And ever-growing laundry piles.

And it was a brief,

Oh so painfully brief life,

Of cleaning, praying and… dreaming.

I wanted to go into nursing

And find a suitable man to be my Noble Squire.

But my kidneys flamed up and I started to pee blood.

Come to my lonely grave sometime, my friend.

I'm off in the corner here.

Forgotten and covered in the ivy.

I lie here in my casket in the dark

Please visit me here in the shadows,

So I can hear you breathing.

## POEM 8

# EDWARD COFFIN
# 1865–1905

There was nothing I could do.

Absolutely nothing because God had spoken.

I tried my hardest to save my little girl's life.

But try as I did,

There was no stopping the stopping

Of her fragile young heart.

My precious daughter saw for the last time

The dilating sunrise that morning in 1889,

From behind the exhilarating rise

Of the Puente Hills to the east.

And when stubborn Helios found his niche

In the apex of the azure sky that day,

My sweet Sophia smiled and said:

"Look papa, I can ride fast."

And down shady Friends Street she rode Stormy,

Her bouncing black steed with ears pricked.

And then I blinked

And Sophia,

My precious sweet Sophia,

Left this Earth in a heartbreaking heap.

I buried my girl on a cloudy morning in March,

And try as I did,

## THE VOICES FROM CLARK CEMETERY

I couldn't control the flood of remembrance

Inside the wellsprings of my screaming soul…

Of my baby girl running up to me on Friends street

Running up to me and jumping into my arms, and saying:

"I love you papa. I love you papa."

After that, I too died… on the inside,

And sought heaven's grace in a bottle.

No one knew about my secret savorings.

No one knew that I dozed off to sleep every night

As drunk as Falstaff.

Not even my wife knew of my private libations

And toasts to an absurd life

Lived in abject sadness.

I lie in bitter repose now in Clark Cemetery,

Next to my sweet precious Sophia.

The worms now tickle us

At the soles of our stilled feet,

Feet we once used while running,

Running together in the wild wind,

Running freely in the mustard fields

Of this quiet Quaker town.

POEM 9
# CHLOE BROADBENT STILLBORN 1899

My simple soul, my eyes,

Have never beheld the jewel of the night,

The morning star that ushers in

The dawning of a new day.

My brief inner heartbeat has never felt

The gentle pelting of the rain,

As it descends downward

Gently, peacefully, magically,

Like the mist of a cascading waterfall

Hidden deeply

Far away

Somewhere in the distance

In the mysterious grottos and crevices

Created by God,

My only friend.

Dearest mother.

Although we were together for those nine months,

I never knew you.

My simple soul, my eyes,

Never beheld your soul, and your eyes.

And although you held me,

I never held you.

Citizens of Earth:

You have no idea.

You have no idea.

POEM 10
# ELVIN ALLEN
# 1889–1905

They were like iron trees!

Hundreds of them!

Poking and piercing their way into the sun-lit sky,

Like moist fingers

Testing the wind direction to the east.

I was born into this Quaker town on Bright Street.

If you take a left from Broadway ,

You will see it

Our little white house with the dormer gables

And the shaded front porch

Where dad and mom sat on hot summer afternoons

Reading the Bible

And knitting my sister's soft sweaters for winter time.

And we all sipped cold lemonade,

In glasses that twinkled in the sun.

I loved baseball.

And I loved hiking in the hills there

To the east.

Where I hunted squirrels and jackrabbits

With my taut leather sling.

And I kissed Belva there.

Then on the day I died,

## THE VOICES FROM CLARK CEMETERY

I decided to climb one of them,

One of those iron fingers,

One of those hundreds of oil derricks

That sucked black crude from the hollow ground,

There in the eastern hills.

I almost made it to the top that day,

Inching slowly slowly slowly

Up  the side wooden ladder,

But I lost my footing nevertheless

And fell to my death at age 16.

And now here I rest

Waiting by this old rotting oak tree,

Here in Clark Cemetery,

Waiting for my bodily resurrection,

And thirsting, forever thirsting

For one more twinkling glass

Of mom's cold lemonade.

POEM 11

# TILLIE LYDSTON
# 1843–1905

I was forty six

When I first saw the hills.

Those most magical eastern hills of my home.

I loved Whittier as my mother

And it saddens me I can't be there again.

I left behind family and friends in faraway Illinois

For those wondrously beautiful eastern hills,

Where my new friends set up homes and feasted

With many songs of worship to our Lord.

On Sundays we all sang loudly and earnestly

In the sun's benevolent rays of the Friends Church.

Gathering all our voices together into one enormous crescendo,

We celebrated the presence of God.

My gift was music

And to God I offered up my singing voice in praise,

And this I did for 41 years.

During apple blossom time in '69

I married Samuel

And he stood by me

As I grew old, got fat and decided to leave Illinois.

When we reached here by train,

Me and Samuel set up the business on Greenleaf,

## THE VOICES FROM CLARK CEMETERY

And made our home

Amidst the whispering cedars and pines on Pilgrim Way.

I bore two children in the upstairs bedroom,

Amidst the doilies and the teacups,

And I heard the voices of heaven

Reveal the truth of a thousand questions.

I died with my Bible

And my head propped on a pillow.

Here in Clark Cemetery

I feel no death,

Just continuing life.

Amidst the singing voices of the dead.

DIGESTED BY THE DUST

POEM 12
# EDWIN VAN DUSEN
# 1831–1903

Come closer my friend

Come closer to my forgotten grave,

Here in Clark Cemetery.

You'll find me enclosed beneath the hardened dirt here,

Beneath the grassy terrain.

My soul enveloped in infinite dust,

Remains alive still.

I fondly remember Christmas time

And hunting birds of prey in Turnbull.

But now I sleep in this eternal death world,

In the eye of Orpheus

Staring downward ever downward

My eye lids inside this cushioned casket,

Flutter and wink again and again,

Wanting love

Or the beginning of an amazing thought.

The thought that I lived and loved,

That I experienced every day of my life

With a mad joy.

POEM 13

# NELLIE GRAY HOLLAND
# 1885–1899

I was never aware of the clock ticking

Or the spring spreading of the rose bud in my mother's green garden.

I never saw the moonrise on a gray October night,

Or tasted the tart fruit of first love.

I never heard the cry of my baby

Or felt the warm heartbeat of a husband next to mine.

For birthdays and holidays

I lit the candles,

A dozen scented red candles,

And watched the ghostly shadows flicker on the walls

Of my mother's special sitting room.

Shadows that danced and swayed and galloped.

Shadows that understood me

And listened to me.

They knew of my weak diseased heart

And of my impending early exit from Earth.

Clark Cemetery is beautiful in the fall.

The owls in the trees screech loudly

And the western winds make a music only I can hear.

My friend, will you kindly light a candle for me?

I am in the dark here

And I wish to see the dancing shadows again.

DIGESTED BY THE DUST

POEM 14
# JESSE FORBES
# 1893–1911

Black Canyon.

Now, there was a place to be!

It is true I was born a brute in a Quaker Town.

Born a bad-tempered brute of a boy

In the two-room digs on Bailey Street and Comstock..

My father fathered two other families,

Unbeknownst to his wife..

And I was the first one disowned.

But my father was a great believer,

And I loved the man like a fool.

I took up the milkin' business at fourteen,

And made my morning way from Orange Drive down to Penn Street.

Delivering the dozens of clinking milk bottles.

Delivering the dozens of morning salutations,

To neighbors and friends in the glad and dismal days.

I had but one romantic interlude in my short stay,

Just one futile attempt at Carpe Diem.

But was left slapped and standing by a disheveled Ethel Hurst

There in the dark shade of Black Canyon

That inauspicious August day in 1910.

Ethel Hurst did not accept the entreaties of a 17 year old brute.

Did not accept my wild stares

Or my insanely puckered lips.

It was to my surprise that I died.

Died so young and so unready.

Still desiring the perfumed kisses of Ethel Hurst,

Still desiring her heart-quenching embraces,

There, in the dark shade of Black Canyon.

POEM 15
# AMANDA THING
# 1829–1918

BF and me

We rode into this muddy enclave,

This Quaker paradise high on an ever-descending hill

In March of '87

With Sunshine, our roan mare,

And a wagon full of old belongings and new hopes.

I recall the mustard fields blooming that spring

Like a million fires in the firmament,

And these fiery fields were intensely difficult to plow.

And the land had to be carved up like slaughtered meat

To pave the way for the railroad

And the first automobiles from Detroit.

First time I saw one,

I almost fainted.

BF and me

We spent many an afternoon in our feathered buggy instead

With Sunshine, our roan mare,

Riding the newly paved roads,

From Rideout's Driveway to County Road.

And we saw,

From the top of Friends Street

The distant Catalina Island,

## THE VOICES FROM CLARK CEMETERY

Shrouded in the hazy Pacific,

Like a sleeping giant under a brown blanket,

And we gasped at the mystical beauty of it

From our hilltop perch.

When BF died of a stroke in '07,

I buried him in Clark Cemetery

And I thought I would never survive the grief.

But God sustained me as always

And I lived eleven more years by myself,

Among the roses and tulips

Of my Whittier Avenue cottage.

At 89 I died an old and tired lady,

More than ready to meet my sweet Savior.

My funeral was grand indeed!

They put baby roses on my casket,

And said the Lord's Prayer.

Then they put me next to BF.

POEM 16

# SOLOMON COOK
# 1820–1900

It was a miracle.

I entered this wicked world with

Mother's umbilical wrapped around my neck like a noose,

Inside a cold cabin made of stone.

My mother,

A beauty of burden,

Chopped the wood

And served chicken neck soup on special occasions.

My father taught me stories from the Bible

And swatted my behind with a strap

If I slept in past 6.

My eight siblings and me

Worked the fields from the rise of Phoebus at dawn

To the fall of the day's eye at twilight,

And we barely had enough to eat,

Except after the harvest.

I taught myself to read at ten years old

And as a young man

I travelled by steamer as a swabby

To Europe, Asia and Africa

And I took in the local colors like one of Twain's tramps.

I met many women of questionable reputation

## THE VOICES FROM CLARK CEMETERY

In many exotic ports-of-call.

But my one true love was my wife of 42 years;

My lovely and patient Pearl.

By train and stagecoach

We came to this quiet Quaker town in 1892,

And lived in the white Queen Anne on Olive Street.

Pearl and me walked on many a Sunday morning

To services at First Christian,

Shaped like a cross,

And together we smelled the gardenia blossoms

In Pastor Crain's eccentric garden.

Why, my Lord, did I have to live so long?

Why did I have to watch my wife and friends die before me?

And why, my Lord, was it a simple cold

That finally stopped my old lived-in heart?

And now I am resting in peace at Clark Cemetery

Under the sprawling sultan-like fronds;

Under the magnificent golden nucleus

Of a single desert palm.

POEM 17
# ETHEL HURST
# 1889–1918

I saw the town rise up

Like a single blade of grass after a spring rain.

I played a multitude of hop-scotch games

With my best friend Hannah on Penn Street.

And sipped a hundred ice cream sodas in the Mercantile at sunset.

My mother took me to Jacob's Grocery every Monday

And it was I who picked the plump oranges

From the big rickety crate.

On Saturdays we worked the fields at Strong's Ranch,

Harvesting the pampas in the walnut fields.

And on Halloween I was the girl in the moon-face costume

for five straight years.

When Christmas brought its luminous lights to the town,

Mother dressed me in red with a bell on my bonnet.

And father sang the carols with a guitar and a tambourine.

I graduated from the big high school in 1907

And in celebration,

Rode my bicycle to Bassett

Still in my starched graduation petticoats.

Jesse Forbes,

He being five years younger than I,

Was the love of my brief stay on this earth.

# THE VOICES FROM CLARK CEMETERY

But when he ventured to steal a kiss that day in Black Canyon,

I used my calloused hand to convey my stern disagreement.

But what wild regrets I've entertained since Jesse drowned that day.

In the wild currents by Pio Pico's crumbling Adobe,

His body bobbing like a sea bird

In the punishing plume of that old deep river.

Beyond the muddy banks and the wild flowers,

Jesse Forbes left this life with a surprised frozen grin.

Why Jesse? Why?

You never knew the truth, my love.

You never really understood what I meant

When I said nothing.

I said No to you when I said nothing that day in Black Canyon,

But I really meant Yes.

The influenza incinerated my heart and soul

With a 106 temperature in the winter of 1918.

Twenty nine years I dare say

Is nothing in terms of eternal life!

I had so much more to do!

I had so much more to dream about!

I walked and talked on the streets of my town,

And on the funeral-dark avenues of my innocent days.

And I planned and I schemed

And all for nothing!.

Indeed, I felt the pulse of fleeting time

And the never-ending,

## DIGESTED BY THE DUST

Ever-turning circle of endless days.

But now I rest here in Clark Cemetery…a virgin corpse

Flirting shamelessly with the bow-tie worms,

Still wild with regrets.

And forever haunted in reverse

By the same recurring memory

Of Jesse Forbes holding a rose.

Under the old oak tree in Black Canyon..

POEM 18

# PERCIVAL JORDAN
# 1892–1912

I am where I am

Because of who I was.

I imbibed a million breaths

And observed the stars dotting the night skies

Like actors taking the stage for another eternal encore.

I am in the air

As I am in the ground.

And I know the truth now.

Life was an impossible possibility.

Born of pleasure and fear and desperation.

And I'm relieved the ridiculous race is over.

I spent most of my carefree days here in Clark Cemetery.

Helping Artilissa water the flowers.

And as a boy I played amidst the sunken graves.

I sat in silence like a scheming spider

Under the stretching shadows of the old tombstones.

I wrote poems to the dead

And read the Psalms aloud

With my many lady friends dressed in silk

Sitting scandalously close to me.

Under a darkening full moon shade one evening

I kissed Ethel Woodstock on the lips

And I released my emerging manhood

With a simmering sigh.

I felt strangely odd when Ethel died that night,

Enveloped in her mother's helpless embrace.

I placed a rose bud upon her mahogany casket

And I cried as a light rain descended

Upon the drinking gorged ground around us..

Indeed I was the annoying little boy in the graveyard;

That flim-flaming rascal

With the cocky smirk of a broken gentleman.

With costumed enterprise,

I tricked many a passerby

With repeated low-moaning dirges

From behind the Hadley tombstone.

Their screams were hilarious but they never caught me.

God knows I had plans.

Plans to be a lawyer.

Plans to be an electrician.

Plans to be married and to find peace of mind.

But when I awoke one cold morning in 1912,

My bed was soaked in warm blood,

And all my plans were forever harvested by the Grim One.

I love Clark Cemetery in the autumn.

When the leaves turn dark and deadly.

When the rippling landscape illuminates the truth

and finality of all things.

## THE VOICES FROM CLARK CEMETERY

Life is just a fast-moving storm

And none of us has the time to notice the returning rainbow.

Oh, for a simple cup of coffee again!

## POEM 19

# LULA PICKERING
# 1887–1906

Have you seen my bluebirds today?

Have you fed them a few crumbs of stale rye bread?

I must have taken a hundred walks as a young girl

In search of my freewheeling friends.

And with only my slender shadow at my side,

I recited a million silent invocations to my Lord.

I greeted the noon tide on those many happy occasions

As if in flight myself.

And my only friends,

Regaled in flying blazing blue,

Flew with me to fantastic heights

And I kissed the rising sun a hundred times

But received not even a smiling sigh in return.

And it was in Black Canyon

That I discovered the one true answer to my only question in life.

I discovered that love is a clinging cloud

That arrives and sometimes lingers.

Or it is a cloud that moves on quickly

Like a late train to Los Angeles in 1904

Leaving only a faint wisp of windy dust in its wake.

Roscoe Settle was that cloud;

A cloud at once full of light and rare beauty.

## THE VOICES FROM CLARK CEMETERY

A cloud that stood still and refused to wink or budge.

But I gave Roscoe Settle my pursed lips

And like a silly infatuated fool

I gave him the hidden treasure within my bosom.

God knows that I pleaded and begged like a panhandling maniac

For my handsome boy to stay.

To stay forever with me in this town of sensational sunsets

And of soaring spiraling bluebirds

In search of a lonely jilted girl

Who now walks as an ethereal restless ghost

Amongst the crosses and stone lilacs of this dead land.

Only my parents knew of my untimely demise.

Only the sheriff and Mr. White knew that I took my own life.

And that I ended my life over Roscoe Settle.

I found the old rope in my father's barn

And the last thing I remember

Was the quick snap of the rope

And of my soft svelte neck

As I threw myself,

Noosed and sad

From my father's hay loft

On a moonless August evening.

POEM 20
# GEORGE W. TOWNE
# 1847–1899

From Iowa I came by restless wagon train.

From the mid-west I arrived

With satchel and silken scalp still intact.

I read Proverbs and Ecclesiastes to pass the time.

I read the Gospels of John and Luke.

I read Harriet Beecher Stowe and

I read John Greenleaf Whittier.

I saw the icy Rocky Mountains beckon me to the west

Waving their invisible fluid fingers

Like blond ballerinas in silent ever-moving tableaux.

I saw the railroad snake through the endless golden valleys.

And I saw the muddy roads converge

Under a hundred bee-infested pepper trees.

And it was here in this new colony I found a home

For my wife Fannie and our three dubious children.

You could always spot me in the distance,

Walking down Pickering Street.

For I was the dapper one in black derby hat

Taking the cash in the Greenleaf Avenue millinery.

I was the suited one in dusty black,

Winking and bowing to the lovely ladies

Showing my respect but imagining something else

## THE VOICES FROM CLARK CEMETERY

Deep within my empty searching soul.

I was the tall, cleanly shaven erudite

Who had memorized the entire Gospel of John

And walked the northern foothills at sunset

Wearing my ever-present derby hat

And meeting, yes,

Secretly meeting Lucy Swain

Under the tall cedar tree on Rideout Ranch.

Confession is indeed good for the soul.

Confession has always allowed a good but dishonest man

to sleep soundly.

To sleep long languorous hours on a cold winter's night.

To sleep for an eternity without guilt or regrets

Under the hardened forgotten dirt of Clark Cemetery.

For I was the handsome one in derby hat

And only Lucy and I knew,

Only she and I knew intimately

About the patch of soft carpet-like grass,

There under the tall silent cedar tree

On Rideout Ranch.

POEM 21
# MITCHELL BUSH
# 1864–1906

When the crash of '89 came I had a nervous breakdown.

Every day I desired suicide.

Every single day I lived in mental anguish.

I know firsthand what the word trouble means.

I know firsthand what it is to be paralyzed by abject fear;

A soul-numbing fear that lurks in the crawlspace of hell

Like an unseen beast ready to strike and kill.

And I know categorically what financial debt is.

I have seen myself as a trapped rat in a deep bottomless pit.

A groveling insanely hopeless and worthless rat

Buried alive inside a smothering grave-like cave.

A suffocating collapsing cave

With no exit or hopeful escape

Praying on my knees to God almighty,

Praying for relief and deliverance

Praying, ever praying, for just one bright hopeful light

In a universe of drowning darkness.

When the bad times hit

I lost my mind and I lost my job.

And worst of all, I lost my humble cottage on College Street.

And when my sweet wife vacated with the two children,

I cried an ocean of tears that have yet to dry;

An ocean of brine that can still be seen

From the airy heights of my town.

Dear Living Ones of today.

Know that I understand.

Know that I went through the same fire;

The same sucking quicksand.

And know that I had to bid the devil good morning.

As you now must.

And finally, please know that I am at rest now.

My eternal reward coming to me at the age of 42.

I was sitting at the dining table at suppertime

When my heart stopped cold.

And at my funeral here in Clark Cemetery,

My estranged wife appeared in ironic black,

And cried an ocean of tears,

That have yet to dry.

DIGESTED BY THE DUST

POEM 22
# HENRIETTA TWEEDY
# 1886–1907

I was always taught that good news puts fat on the bones.

And I was taught by my strict Christian father

That before honor comes true humility.

I remember picking the Valencia's one summer afternoon

And hearing him say

That the winners in life are the givers,

And that a foolish man always despises his mother.

And after services on Sundays,

I can still remember all of us congregated

In the sparse dining room

There on California Street,

Eating mother's delectable starchy dinners

With my father in white starched shirt

Saying the "grace" before meals,

And ending the prayer, saying:

"A soothing tongue is a tree of life."

I loved life and I loved God.

And that is all I can say

Here in my lonely grave.

Except,

Roscoe Settle was a thief.

He was the thief of my heart and of my soul.

He was the only one for me.

And I was the only one for him

And that's the God's honest truth.

We met on a Thursday evening at dusk in 1904

And his lips found my lips

His blue gentle eyes healed my spiritual blindness

Like Christ by the well

When he met her,

The thirsty woman from Samaria.

And I saw him on the road to Montebello Heights that long ago day

And little did I know it then,

That would be the last time

I was to see Roscoe Settle alive.

Pray for me all kindred souls of the day.

Pray for me as I set loose the atoms

Of a million milliseconds of human time.

Life demands nothing from us

Except,

To die.

It is the ultimate act of humility.

It is the ultimate act of final humanity.

And I am truly honored now

As the worms greedily gnaw

Upon the fat of my bones.

# DIGESTED BY THE DUST

POEM 23

# BURR MCCLELLAND
# 1859–1932

I built the wooden fences

That lined the homesteads of a thousand acres.

And I rode the ponies to move the beef and the bovine

Through Arkansas and Abilene.

I lived wild and free.

A brother to the dust and the dirt and the debris

Of untamed, impervious youth.

I wielded a pick-axe

In the infant days of this Quaker town.

And did my part

In building the East Whittier Ditch

Across Sycamore Canyon.

And I was there with a shovel

When the Hybrid Tree on County Road

Found its rooted Jerusalem

With the petunias and the azaleas.

I was there in the pelting rain

With Belle and my black umbrella

When they dedicated the new Carnegie Library

On dusty old Greenleaf Avenue in 1907.

And I was standing and waving

When Thomas Alva Edison rode by on parade

# THE VOICES FROM CLARK CEMETERY

That overcast day in 1915.

God knows I worked hard and sweated all my life.

And God also knows

I never turned down an honest job that came my way.

I married Belle when I was 17

And sired four rambunctious children in the 1880's.

Were they a blessing or were they my cross to bear in life?

I'm dead now so I can't answer that question.

But while still breathing, I survived

Pneumonia, diphtheria and scarlet fever

And I lost my left pinkie finger one icy morning

While sawing the firewood in the winter of 1891.

God knows I lived a long and happy life.

But I was ready to die when I died.

Step closer dear sentient being of planet Earth.

Will you bring me a petunia?

To place upon my solemn forgotten grave?

You might find some still.

Growing like children who never grow old.

Under the calming shade of the Hybrid Tree.

POEM 24
# MINNIE FINCH
# 1879–1900

Piano music.

Harmoniously flowing piano music.

And then…

When my soul closed its soft portal to life and love,

My mother was gently fingering the piano ivories.

The smooth lovely alabaster keys

Of the black mahogany piano.

The one inside our small but quaint

Broadway street parlor room.

The one my father had delivered

As a yuletide gift in 1896.

The one my mother played every night.

The wondrously euphonic strains of Bach, Mozart

And the brilliantly dazzling Beethoven.

I especially loved the Moonlight Sonata

And every night while my mother played

I read the Bronte Sisters by candle light.

I truly thought like a fool

That I was a Galapagos turtle

That would live to a ripe old age in the sun.

But alas,

My appendix burst

While hoofing it on the tranquil trails of Turnbull Canyon.

With Walter Cummings at my side.

He held my hand as I fainted slowly away.

My exiting soul

Like a boat leaving the starry harbor at midnight.

Watching the evaporation of the universe before my eyes.

Then I heard it inside my closing collapsing mind.

Beethoven's Moonlight Sonata.

My swan song for timeless eternity.

DIGESTED BY THE DUST

POEM 25

# HARVEY DENNING
# 1909–1923

"I saw the universe a thousand times."

I saw the face of God

Spread out across the sky

Like a million cities on fire.

Like Troy cut into little pieces

By the slashing sword of Achilles.

Cut to shreds and bleeding.

There on the ramparts

There inside the fissures and crevices

Of ten thousand unknown dreams.

I read the stories of Homer

And the tales of a thousand and one Arabian nights.

And I read the solemnly immortal words

Of Longfellow, Poe and Defoe.

And I decided inside my mind long before I died

To perhaps write the greatest story ever told.

But I fell from my tree house

There on Dorland Street

There in the cool shadows of the walnut tree.

What would have been my story I wonder.

What visions would I have conjured

For all to read and envision?

## THE VOICES FROM CLARK CEMETERY

My friend, will you write my story now?

Will you take pen in hand and possess my voice?

Will you find the noble courage to speak for me?

This forgotten dead soul

Buried here in the dark dust of Clark Cemetery?

If you kindly consent,

Please begin it with these words:

"I saw the universe a thousand times."

POEM 26
# LUCY SWAIN
# 1861–1896

Lies! Lies! All damnable lies!

I know the injustice of malicious gossip.

I know the outrage of a loose evil tongue.

In life, I was Lucy Swain, the maligned!

I was Lucy Swain, the indignant!

In truth, I was Lucy Swain, the law-abiding, god-fearing victim

Who resided over on Milton Avenue

With her bent-over heart-broken mother.

In fact, I was Lucy Swain, the innocent weeping victim

Of a thousand cruel hypocritical stares.

And so, let me shout it out

As loudly as my silent soul can,

From my deep grave here in Clark Cemetery:

I never set foot, not once, on Rideout Ranch!

I never set eyes on the winking blue orbs

Of the devastatingly handsome George Towne,

That philandering cad with the fine derby hat.

I never tasted the warm pulsating kisses

from his sweet-tasting, pursed lips.

And I never felt the caressing electric touch

Of his firm groping fingers upon my bosom,

There, under the old cedar tree on Rideout Ranch!

## THE VOICES FROM CLARK CEMETERY

Lies! All lies!

And as God is my witness

I never spent even one gloriously romantic moment

In the embrace of the incredibly strong arms

Of the sexy man married to Fannie Towne!

Amen!

POEM 27
# CECIL SHARPLESS
# 1893–1904

On the day he died,

My father gave me his gold watch.

I was ten and I too was dying.

The doctor said I had a diseased heart,

But I think it was my father's death that killed me.

But to be honest,

Life was too short and too strange for me.

As a Quaker boy, I worshipped God

With solemn eyes uplifted.

And as a normal growing boy,

I found out about the fascinating mysteries of love

With curious eyes staring straight ahead.

My next door neighbor, Roscoe Settle,

Played interesting games in his backyard

That I did not quite understand.

But I must truthfully say,

I think old maid Nelson is a very charming lady!

Mother, please come get me.

I dislike the dirt and the darkness here.

I want to come home and sit in my room once again,

And stare out my wide open window.

I wish to see what new interesting games Roscoe Settle is playing today.

Father, thank you for the watch.

But time, Father Time, has ceased to be for me,

Like my diseased deceased heart.

POEM 28

# WALTER CUMMINGS
# 1873–1904

Being alive had its ups

And being dead has its downs.

But alas, I do not mind it so much.

Being dead means you're not in debt to the Mercantile anymore!.

And that is most good!

Now I'm just ambitiously rotting here,

In the worm-laden soil of Clark Cemetery,

Now completely in debt to God almighty!

In the summers, the folks from town

Come walking down the shadowed lanes

With roses and lilies in gloved hands

Mumbling muted words that mean nothing to me now.

Not far from my eternal bed here,

I can hear the mellifluously singing voice of sweet Minnie Finch.

Oh, how she used to love music!

And oh, how I loved to sit with her,

In the old papered parlor room

Of her slatted white house on Broadway Street!

And listen….shhh…listen to her mother play "Moonlight Sonata"

On the big black piano.

Those sky blue eyes of hers melted my heart

Like ice cream in August.

Like Adam in the penetrating gaze of his lover.

And I fell in love with her.

The night we kissed on the front porch veranda.

The night she gave me her hair ribbon made of silk.

On that horrible afternoon when she died,

She was in excruciating pain

From our hike in the canyon.

I held her weakened hand in mine

And as my sweet Minnie Finch closed her eyes for the last time,

I said: "Sing to me. Please sing to me."

And now she is, over there

By the stately desert palms,

Her clear ethereal voice intoning Amazing Grace.

And I will forever be amazed

That I loved so delightful a woman,

So delightful and beautiful, a flower.

POEM 29
# LOTTIE GORDON
# 1884–1907

It was my ultimate goal in life

To marry my magnificent man

In the magnificent Friends Church.

It was my profound destiny in life

To wear white with pink forget-me-nots

In my curled cascading hair

In the stained glass resplendence

Of the magnificent Friends Church.

It was my dream in life

To honor my handsomely honorable husband

With a son and daughter

And to live in the gracious grace of God

As a happy humble woman

In my own happy humble house

On a tree-lined street in this magnificent Quaker town!

And it was my supreme honor

To be escorted to the magnificent Friends Church

On the loving arm of my lionhearted stalwart

On all those Sunday mornings in the sun of my youth

In the sweltering summer of 1906!

Roscoe Settle, I knew,

Was sent by my Lord to me,

To be my honorable husband and my champion!

Then, he died.

My soul still spasms with profound pain

Over the demise of my magnificent man.

It seemed half the town turned out for the burial,

Here in Clark Cemetery.

I lived on one more year

And died of pneumonia on a cold January morning.

I could no longer bear to breathe

Without my lionhearted stalwart,

Without my handsomely honorable husband, to be.

My only reason for living.

POEM 30
# B. F. THING
# 1830–1907

Longevity is a by-product of remaining quiet.

Good sense is the precursor to a life

Filled with sustainable surprises.

Christian patience is the result

Of pricking one's thumb one too many times

In one's burgeoning rose garden.

And a healthy heart is the reward

For always allowing one's wife

To have her indomitable way.

But alas, my finest moments as a man

Were spent with a woman.

And my finest moments with Amanda,

My ornery but assiduous wife, and better half,

Occurred with a horse in halter chains.

Dear friends,

Would you like to see the sunset at a ripe old age?

Would you like to enjoy life without ulcers, fears or regrets?

Would you like to be on the receiving end

Of a thousand respectful smiles?

Then, my friends,

I would advise you

To always remember to never forget.

And above all,

Never be in a hurry to slow down!

Thank you, Lord Jesus,

For dying on the rugged old cross

For the remission of a multitude of sins.

And thank you, "Old Hateful,"

For never requiring any "thank you's"

In all those years we lived together

As husband, and ornery wife!

## POEM 31

# BEULAH GROTON
# 1886–1890

I remember the adoring eyes of my mother

And I remember the sweet fragrances

of the orange blossoms in spring.

I can recall the wagging of my dog's tail

And the smell of frying bacon

Inside my mother's kitchen on a Sunday morning.

And I do recall burning up with fever

Inside a washbasin filled with ice.

The day before they buried me here in Clark Cemetery,

My parents gathered friends and family together

At the farm on Washington Street.

And with my little white coffin open,

They posed around my still body and,

My pale sunken face for the keepsake photograph.

They dressed me in white satin

And laid me out under the noon sun.

I don't miss life really

Because my days were few.

But I do miss my dog,

And waking up on Christmas morning.

POEM 32
# WILLIAM FRANKLIN JOHNSON 1915 (ONE HOUR)

I know nothing of the Earth

Or of life as a human being.

I know nothing of spitting watermelon seeds

Or sitting on a pine tree fence at sunset.

I know nothing about a cool rain in summer

Or the warmth of a fireplace on a freezing December night.

I know nothing of love and pain and dreams.

Nothing of pillows or mud puddles,

Nothing of sweet candy or soft ice cream.

But I do know this:

That there is a place we all go to after breathing.

That there is a wondrous realm with spirits aglow

And sights too beautiful to behold.

That there is a loving God the Father

Who smilingly embraces all spirits upon their instant arrival.

That there is a land of love and happiness

That cannot be described with mere human words.

Simple mere words,

Written by an infant boy,

Who only lived one short hour

In his grace!

# DIGESTED BY THE DUST

POEM 33
# AGNES TARAZAS
# 1903–1921

Yo se ojos de odio

Yo se las sonresas de un Corazon falso.

I was baptized at St. Mary of the Assumption,

And I received first Holy Communion there

At age eight in a white dress and veil.

My madre gave me white carnation flowers

And a rosary made of black coffee beans.

And my father blessed me on the forehead

With a kiss and a prayer.

I lived on the outskirts in Jim Town by the railroad tracks.

I knew to stay put, and mind my own business.

I cooked and scrubbed and mended

And I never knew a day off from drudgery.

Oh, it hurts and angers me so!

How my family and me were treated so disrespectfully.

My grave here, in Clark Cemetery, is a cheap one.

My headstone here,

In this old Broadway graveyard,

Is a small cracked forgotten one,

Over-covered with dead weeds and decayed palm fronds.

No one remembers me.

On one ever will.

## THE VOICES FROM CLARK CEMETERY

I am dead now and so is everyone else who ever knew my name.

It's that simple. It's that tragic!

For, yo los ojos de odio

Yo se las sonresas de un Corazon falso.

POEM 34
# DANIEL STREETER
# 1826–1904

When you live as long as I lived.

When you keep breathing day after day after day.

You learn to not take life so seriously.

For alas, in this sensuous garden called Earth,

There are a multitude of flowers and herbs.

Of smooth stones and pungent shrubs and scented briars.

Of wild roses and prickly blackberry thorns.

I recall the faces, both masculine and feminine,

And I remember their words and muted whispers.

Sometimes they barked and beguiled.

And sometimes they hit you full force in the face

With their silent stubborn stares.

But we are all God's children, here in his garden.

And I, for one, was the least with the most.

If I could live only one day over again,

I would choose the day I would have lived.

After I stopped living.

THE VOICES FROM CLARK CEMETERY

**POEM 35**
# LILLIE DOWNS
# 1879–1893

Grandmother Downs wore an old black eye patch.

And with no teeth to speak of

She taught me to skin a rabbit with a dull butter knife.

And it was I, Lillie Downs, late of this Quaker town,

Who painted the long white picket fence on Pickering Street

In the long drowsy summer of 1892.

And it was I, Lillie Downs, the girl with the petunia in her hair,

Who could sing in C sharp as a nine year old

With the sainted choir of adults at First Methodist.

Father was my best friend until 1892.

He walked me to Evergreen Elementary for two years

And together at summer solstice

We rode the train from Norwalk to Los Angeles

To witness the first summer sunset and taste the tacos

at old Olvera Street.

I found him at 4:30 on a March morning

As cold and stiff as a Yukon log.

Grandmother Downs fainted by the brick fireplace.

And I screamed to God for a miracle.

I learned that day that miracles are for the saints

And not the sinners.

Now I rest in this dirt here at Clark Cemetery.

The roots of the walnut trees say good morning to me

With friendly warm handshakes

And humble knees bowed.

POEM 36
# MARY ALICE JONES
# 1862–1903

I was Medusa, gorgon girl with snakes for hair!

Gorgon girl with the killer eyes

That turned all men to statues of stone!

My life was painfully long and pathetically short.

My life covered forty years of tempered tears

and embarrassing humiliations.

Forty years of faithless devotion and endless desires to kill or die!

I must be honest,

For it is true – the best time to be honest - is when you are

at last quite dead!

But I hated church as I hated God!

Not because I didn't believe in him,

Like some fool on a toadstool! No!

But because he didn't believe in me!

For I must ask in screaming intonations:

Why was I born with such a protruding knotted nose?

A nose not fit even for the visage of an arched aardvark!

Why was I born with such crooked ugly teeth?

Teeth not fit even for the jowls of a dumb donkey!

My husband, William Henry Jones, was no husband.

He cashed in my dowry before the setting of the sun on our forced

wedding day.

And I'm sure it was to his intense relief

That I perished in the fire

That forever destroyed my misshapen mandibles.

How lucky I am they planted me here by Citrus Road

With my far-flung feet facing to the eternal east.

The weeds are growing untended above me

And the stars at night are oblivious to my forgotten bones.

I now exult like a fairy tale princess

In the indescribable magical beauty

Of majestic magnificent death!

POEM 37
# LUCIUS K. STAMPS
# 1894–1908

Icarus and Daedalus from Dayton were my life's inspiration.

When in 1903 they flew like fledgling falcons

In the December chill of human history!

My dream, too, was to fly!

To fly high and mighty like them!

To touch the stars with strands of rope and wood.

To touch the eyelids of Jupiter himself

With cool-headed courage

And to be firmly at the controls

Of the winged sandals of the helmeted Hermes!

It was not my destiny to fly however.

Except in my lingering daydreams and secret reveries.

On the last day of my life

I awoke drenched in a feverish sweat.

And the last living thing I remember seeing

Was the ashen face of my tearful mother,

Tearfully praying

Hopelessly praying the Lord's Prayer

In the December chill of my blue-walled bedroom.

## POEM 38
# IDA KINCAID
# 1866–1903

I was Ida Kincaid

Wife of Charles

And mother of a pernicious brood of five sinister sons.

My first born required eighteen hours of excruciating labor,

And I should've known then!

After Charles, our son, finally had his behind swatted

By the venerable Doctor Lont,

Charles, my husband, smoked a relieved cigar

under the willow tree there,

By the front porch of our Milton Street cottage.

My second pregnancy was like the birthing of a butterfly

from its bulging cocoon.

The bloody struggle, I surmised,

Would be my last day on this Earth.

But Doctor Lont

With handkerchief and black bag in tow,

Adroitly saved my life with trembling hands

And a distant stare in his saddened eyes.

Miraculously and stubbornly

I pushed three more squirming boys out of my swollen aching womb,

With the fifth destroying my kidneys.

Charles never knew this,

But I must confess.

Doctor Lont, old Doctor Lont,

Kissed me when Albert first saw the light.

And for a minute there

Old Doctor Lont stopped trembling.

## POEM 39
## GRANT OLMSTEAD
## 1868–1899

Just once.

Just one single sublime moment of love

Is all I ever desired.

All I ever reasonably wanted in life!

Was I not a man with a river of passion

Raging through me, raging with rushing torrents

Rushing madly through the deepest gorges

Of my manly soul?

Was I not a human being with gazing probing eyes

Cursed with blinding sight,

Cursed with confounding appetites for flesh

And incredible intimacies in the dark,

Intimacies even the gods of Olympus had access to

Tons of minutes ago?

And so I ask: What good is a windmill without the wind?

What good is a man's tongue without words to utter

Words of deep intense longings

To the faces of patient pulchritude?

What good are a man's prayers to a dead god

In an empty universe?

Now I'm here in Clark Cemetery,

Still thirsting for one woman's touch,

One woman's thrilling embrace!

Instead, I am tasting the kisses of a thousand worms

Here in the sheets of my bed of death.

Amen to lost love!

POEM 40
# DR. O. S. LONT  MD
# 1822–1893

The proud peacock bird

Knew of my enormous egregious ego.

As a young satyr in suspenders

I sought out the fillies and the mares

In the old town of Springfield.

They allowed me, the boy,

The boy with the full head of coarse brown locks

And brown beard to match,

To entice them to esoteric spots

In the distant cold canyons.

And with precise skill and determined non-chalance,

I stabbed them with my spear, my long hard spear!

Stabbed and pierced them with

The Punto Reverso and the Hai!

And then it all changed.

I saw the sunset of my bachelor days,

And married Melissa.

POEM 41
# MELISSA LONT
# 1825–1911

How does one as low and humble as I

Sum up my life of 86 years

In a mere poem as brief and short-lived

As life itself?

And what is the secret to my long life?

What do I know that you, my friend,

Would like to know

About success and survival?

About good health and good luck?

My answer is this:

Do not complain and do not explain! Never!

And as for being married all those years to Doctor Lont?

Well, truth be known, like Hera,

I knew of my husband's infidelities.

But I also knew to look the other way

And pretend to not see or know!

I admired Ida Kincaid for her sacrifices to maternity.

But I loathed Ida Kincaid for her matrimonial mendacity.

At her funeral in June of 1903

I aloofly stood across the way

There on dusty Broadway Street

Under the bulbous blue jacarandas

Screaming hallelujahs!

As Mr. White lowered her cream-colored coffin into the Netherworld!

And when Doctor Lont, my husband of 41 years,

died of the consumption,

I did not cry nary a tear!

Why should I have?

Now I too am resting within this hard ground next to him.

Next to the man, my man in perpetual suspenders from Springfield,

My man who never ceased being a boy.

POEM 42
# PEDRO REYES
# 1884–1907

I am deceased and that is all.

Salvo, fue quien lo hizo.

And I leave these sayings as a gift,

For the minions and the multitudes.

For I was Pedro Reyes,

Collector of wise saws and practical proverbs:

The last shall be first and the first last…

Never trust the advice of a man in trouble…

The smaller the mind, the greater the conceit…

What sense does it make to throw stones

Into the well that quenches your thirst?…

It is better to be thin and free, than fat and a slave…

Liars aren't believed even when they tell the truth…

There is always someone who is worse off than you are…

And finally,

I loved you Rebecca Estrada.

Even as I did what I did!

I called out to the war muses!

¡Te quiero! ¡Te odio!

Then I realized you had left me,

Left me flat as a pancake on the soapstone,

And when they tried to remove me,

**DIGESTED BY THE DUST**

The white boys in blue,

Little bits of my soul were left on the griddle.

Adios! Adios to you my friends!

Buenos Noches!

## POEM 43
# REBECCA ESTRADA
# 1880–1907

Pendejo!

Thief!

Killer!

Pedro Reyes, le confianza! Pedro Reyes, te amé!

Pedro Reyes, You used me like an old library book.

You opened my pages, but

You never read the words.

Never read the story of my heart

Never comprehended the meanings of my torn soul!

And when I died that day in May,

Your face, your eyes

Bit me like a hundred hungry hounds.

Then they came and picked me up with the White Wagon

And took me to the undertaker's

There on bustling Philadelphia Street.

Yes, took me back like some old used volume,

Unclasped, unbound and unread,

Without a prologue or an epilogue,

The saddest story never told.

POEM 44
# LUTIE M. SAYLES
# 1881–1908

There is an old knotted oak tree,

Venerable and wise as Tiresias himself,

Ancient as the hills and gullies of this Quaker town,

Located behind the Friends College,

There in the eastern heights.

If one were to hike to this tree,

In deference to the snakes and squirrels there,

You will find our carved initials on that old leafy lovely tree.

"LS and "RS,"

Carved with an ivory blade

Inside a jagged heart.

It is true I had his baby.

It is true I knew of his engagement to Lottie Gordon.

And it is true I was just one of his many hornswoggled hens.

But how could I resist the devil?

This blue-eyed Adonis?

This ever-sleeping Endymion?

During the last moment of my short life,

There on shady La Cuarta Street,

I recall feeling the whirring rush of enormous pain

And of enormous relief!

And I knew inherently

That my beautiful baby was traveling on the Road to Damascus.

And then, a blinding light!

Dear orphan child:

My only advice to you is this-

Resist the devil, and he will flee!

POEM 45
# STARLING B. RIGGINS
# 1866–1900

There was not a day that went by

When I didn't think of them:

My departed parents, late of this citrus parish,

Late of this quiet conservative community,

Of walnut trees, churches and dusty country roads,

Of the fervently faithful, and of the decidedly devout.

When they died on the same day in 1895,

Both in bed,

Both of pneumonia

And both in an eternal embrace,

I tried to accept that which I could never accept.

I tried to understand that which I could never hope to understand.

And I tried to grieve over that which I could never be consoled.

On the train back to Chicago for the burial by the big lake,

I stayed with them in the baggage car,

Shivering in the snoring night, and

Sweating tears during the daunting day.

The fourth commandment states:

"Thou shalt honor thy father and thy mother."

God knows I did that as best I could,

And I believed with my heart and shaken soul

That I was to be blessed by the grace of the Lord

With life-long excellent health.

With life-long happiness, and

With life-long prosperity.

But unfortunately for me,

I had the misfortune to lose a fortune.

My mind!

Then on a sultry September evening

I found nirvana with my father's colt pistol.

Dare to venture, my friends, to the old Pumphouse on Walnut Street.

Dare to find the bullet hole by the two-sided door there.

That is where the bullet that killed me

Found rest in the rust and the rebar.

Forgive me God.

I knew not what I was doing!

DIGESTED BY THE DUST

POEM 46
# GEORGE WASHINGTON COLE
# 1827–1911

So here I sleep.

Buried in this dirt.

Covered in this earth.

Returning to the dust.

Finding heaven in the whispers of the wind.

And as for all my friends here,

All these stilled silent voices of Clark Cemetery,

We represent just a single sand pebble

Just a minute solitary dust particle

In an ever expanding infinite universe

Of shadows and scant tracings.

Travel to any city or town in the United States,

Or any sovereign country on Terra Firma,

And you will find the endless names of us,

The dead,

Who lived and died since the onset

Of the Gilded Age of Bessemer steel.

And those endless lists of the dead are nothing,

Nothing in comparison to the endless lists

Of the by-gone personages before us,

The past generations,

Who breathed and sighed and spasmed

Since the onset of Eden's first heartbeat.

My friends, we are all so small,

And so minuscule.

Does it not behoove us to dance

Even while the music plays?

Does it not behoove us to be kind,

Even when the cruel day

Finally slaps us on the side of our faces?

So here I sleep.

Buried deep in this forgotten grave

Just a whispering shadow of a former man

Awaiting with baited breath

The blare of the last trumpet!

# DIGESTED BY THE DUST

POEM 47

# BELVA BERRY
# 1889–1905

I truly never asked to be born.

I truly never wanted any of this.

But what choice did I have?

What choice does any one of us have?

With our first breath

We begin our long slow descent into the darkness.

With our last breath

We end this long steady slide

From nothing to nothing

From dust to dust.

I was the girl who lived in the corner house

Over on Newlin and Broadway streets.

I was the shy freckled daughter

Of Lunetta and James Berry.

And I was the unknown silent witness

To the crushing tragic tumble

Of my secret esoteric friend, Elvin.

Elvin Allen.

Elvin and me walked hand in hand

To the eastern hills that day.

Elvin and me stared into each other's eyes and smiled that day.

And Elvin and me dared to dance on the sweet oily dirt that day.

There in the midst of the black fields,

The land of the black oil machines

That rise high like chess pieces

The Bishops of industry and money!

We kissed that day

And it was our first kiss.

And then, he climbed up the ladder there.

I saw him fall,

Fall like a falcon from the heavens.

And I knew he was gone.

Please forgive me God for running away.

Please forgive me God for never telling anyone

Of the first kiss, our kiss,

That long ago day in the black fields

In the eastern hills

Of this Quaker town.

## POEM 48

# CHARLES EPPS
# 1863–1903

It was I, Charles Epps,

The mustached mason with the triumphant trowel,

The bushy browed benefactor

Of my father's farm tools.

It was I who laid the cornerstone

Of the Friends College

There on dusty Painter Street and Philadelphia,

There in the stunning summer shadows

There under the blue confluence of God's amazing mind

His infinite sky of azure mercies.

The smiling ladies made lunch and

The whistling men formed the lines that day!

We worked there, up on that hill,

The hill to the east beyond dusty Painter Street,

Worked there until sunset's yawn.

With rippling muscles sore

And calloused hands splintered,

We erected the future of this Quaker town

With nails, timber and sweaty brows.

My friends, you must come to Clark Cemetery sometime,

And visit the shadows.

We lie here quite alive!

Alive amongst the perennials

Awaiting as forgotten wisps of spirit,

Awaiting God's greatest gift-

The body's resurrection.

## POEM 49
# AUGUSTINA GONZALES
# 1893–1907

They call me the Dead Mexican Princess!

They called me the Rio Grande Water Lilly!

Truth be known –

My family was here long before the white man.

My family was here when the mustard blooms

brought envy from the sun!

My people farmed this land

Long before the foul furrows of the English and the Irish.

Years and decades before the guns and the lies!

My people are buried in this land.

Buried long before the ridicule and the insults.

Can you hear our robust music?

Taste our robust recipes?

We expect no gratitude, just respect.

They call me the Dead Mexican Princess.

I rode here on horseback from Mexico at ten.

I lived by the river near the Pio Pico marshes.

Lived as a poor princess

But rich in family and faith!

I died of a fever on the eve of Easter.

Now buried here.

Perhaps buried with a Water Lilly atop my grave.

POEM 50
# NEWTON W. MOON
# 1853–1904

So, what is the truth?

My friend, have you thought deeply about life?

Have you thought long and hard about the endless ticking of time

Have you pondered and mused and ruminated

with all your mind and soul?

I have lain on many an afternoon

Under the old cedar on Rideout Ranch

And I have reckoned the infinite mercies of the wind.

Have pondered the intrepid ascendance of the sun.

The simple pretense of the flower.

And I have considered the Earth's colossal incessant turning.

Have wondered and contemplated long into the night

The whirling pulling maelstrom of the human dilemma:

To live is to ultimately die!

And so,

What is the truth, my friend?

Why are we here on this huge ball of dust and water and fire?

And where do we go after the body ceases to breathe?

My friend,

Close your eyes!

Close them tightly and never open them again!

And then you will see the truth!

POEM 51

# FLORENCE MCLANE
# 1889–1902

Psst… over here!

My toppled tombstone is the one

With the somber seraph carrying a cross.

My grave is the one that no one can see or find.

My hidden final resting place is in the digesting shade

By the willowy walnut tree.

Can you find me?

Olly olly oxen free!

Do you see me?

Will you now hear me?

I breathed my days on Pasadena Street

Inside the little white house with the horseshoe over the door.

I slept my nights under the stars

With dreams and visions and intense remembrances.

My cross to bear bore no semblance

To the old bloody rugged one

Borne by my Lord and Savior to Golgotha.

To my friends and foes,

Dead now for a multitude of minutes.

I sought no pain or revenge.

But your closed eyes never noticed

My own bloody cumbersome cross.

## THE VOICES FROM CLARK CEMETERY

Never truly noticed the tiny ray of pure light

Deep, deep inside my singed soul.

Enveloped and masticated alive

By the deadening darkness of the faithless.

My final words to you all:

Olly olly oxen Free!

POEM 52
# ERNEST F. GRAVES
# 1899–1900

Earth friends.

Not even one birthday party. Not one!

Therefore, I have only one thing to say:

Don't take it personally.

## POEM 53
# OLIVE FRAZIER
# 1854–1895

To my many august friends,

Mere survivors under this hungry consuming California sky.

Before you can reach high to the stars, my friends,

Both feet must firmly be set upon the ground first.

This, in essence, is the lesson of a lifetime.

Here in Clark Cemetery, the soil is rich and fertile.

In my prime years I have walked here

Walked on many an afternoon and many an early evening.

Walked and slowly strolled and ambled

Like a solitary tumbleweed in a restless wind.

Like a knock-kneed crab in a dark watery place

Commiserating with the barnacles.

It was on such a stroll

That I encountered the handsome Mr. Frazier.

Milton by name, bricklayer by trade.

We watched the sunset that evening.

Two hawks in flight high in the blue

Swaying effortlessly in the high breeze.

We found love in the dust

And we found heartbreak in the endless shadowed distances

Of Clark Cemetery.

I left this earth giving birth to my baby.

And now together we peacefully reside in this deep hole.

Together with Milton, my love.

Together now and forever in the dirt and the dust.

Milton, I am sorry I left you alone when I died.

So sorry you had to go on without us.

Often when the clouds above give drink to this dead land,

I think of us

Wondrously and miraculously alive,

Strolling to the east under the canopy of the walnut trees.

Your hand in mine

Your heart and mine intermingling magically.

Thank you my husband.

I was indeed privileged to be your wife.

POEM 54

# MILTON FRAZIER
# 1845–1899

There is nothing worse or more cruel.

Nothing more insidious or dastardly

Than losing a wife and child

On the same day and at the same hour.

Imagine losing your entire family

Between the rising and the setting of the sun.

Imagine sitting helplessly by your beloved's bed

Awaiting the safe arrival of your only child.

And imagine your child coming into this world

Still and stiff and vacant.

And then, imagine your precious wife closing her eyes

For the last time and ceasing to breathe.

It cannot be described in words–

The punishing pain the unbelievable agony–

It is the ultimate heartbreak.

The worst part was picking her burial dress, and then,

Burying them both in the same casket–

On that sunny September morning.

But I am with them now, happily

And at peace, finally.

As with all flesh,

I died my death four years later.

## DIGESTED BY THE DUST

Not of natural causes, no.

But of loneliness. Plain and simple.

For I was but a single insignificant rock

In the middle of a nowhere desert, and

There was no longer any purpose for my existence.

My friends, you can find us by the Dorland Street entrance.

There is a rusty gate there.

When you see the first desert palm,

Turn right and go ten yards to the west.

Our graves are the ones with the crabgrass overtaking them.

If you could see us,

You would notice that our toes are facing eastward.

Our faces are scouting the clouds, and

Our silent, muted voices are trolling the stars.

Living life, my friends, is like erecting a brick wall.

One brick at a time, one day at a time.

Go to the Harvey House on Painter Street

And you will see one of my brick walls.

I invite you to see my handiwork… my legacy to this Quaker town!

Look to the corner stone there.

And you will see my father and my mother and my three sisters.

They are ghosts like me now in this haunted old graveyard.

Look to the mortar there at Harvey House.

And you will also find

The stuff of my vanished dreams.

POEM 55

# RUTH HELEN UHRIG
# 1888–1908

I remember the Indian summers most of all.

The drowsy balmy days of late September and early October.

I remember the calming chorus of the trees,

Especially here in Clark Cemetery,

With the benign wind caressing the still branches,

Teasing and tickling the leaves,

Performing masterfully,

The silent music of a thousand lazy afternoons.

Listen. Can you hear it?

And I recall that afternoon in 1903

While standing under the shady pepper tree,

Here in Clark Cemetery

That moment of sweet virginal bliss.

That long-forgotten one second in time,

When that blue-eyed fox named Roscoe

Kissed me, a mere girl of 15, on the lips.

There, on the threshold to my very soul!

Oh, the true joys of life are so simple and so fleeting!

And finally,

To my friends in old Whittier town,

I discovered after my demise that,

There is a happy way to die and a sad way to die.

And it will all depend on how well you treated people while alive.

Thankfully, I died the happy way.

In my sleep.

Dreaming of the silent music,

On a long-ago afternoon in September,

Under the old shady pepper tree,

Here in Clark cemetery.

POEM 56
# MARCUS SETTLE
# 1845–1906

We arrived here in 1892 from Joplin Missouri.

We moved in next door to the Sharpless clan,

There on south Penn Street by the newly-laid railroad tracks.

By train we came, my wife, children and grandchildren,

Poised to work and to begin life anew.

My best friend is and was Jesus Christ.

The Alpha and the Omega!

The Lion from the Tribe of Judah!

The Everlasting One!

The Prince of Peace!

And even with this firm faith,

My son yet found sin,

In the secret sunsets of this Quaker community.

Faithful friends, judge me not.

Cast not a stone towards me.

For I never was untrue to Josie, my loyal wife.

Never unresponsive to the earthly needs of my family.

And never at a loss of loving praise

For my sweet Savior!

You must know the truth about Roscoe, my friends.

He was indeed the obvious target.

But I, the innocent head of the Settle clan,

**DIGESTED BY THE DUST**

One Marcus Settle, late of Joplin Missouri

Found excruciating salvation one June morning

In the hidden tiger whiskers

Surreptitiously immersed

Inside my hot porridge breakfast bowl.

## POEM 57
# HATTIE L. ROGERS
# 1844–1917

The playing cards of life are a stacked deck.

As soon as you begin to breathe

You begin to die and disintegrate.

All of the winners in life

Eventually end up the losers.

You enter this Big House with nothing.

Nothing but a cracked soul, a cursed heart

And that stacked deck of crooked playing cards.

Your destiny, my friends, lies in the dust.

So I figured early on, like King Solomon,

That there is no use; it is all futile and hopeless at best.

When I came to this sad realization

About life on this staggering planet,

I decided the only worthwhile meaning in living

Is in finding true happiness,

Even in the midst of hopeless despair.

Even in the midst of this mocking gaping graveyard

That lusts for flesh and blood

Like Odysseus' giant with the one eye

Like a carnivorous Scylla, hiding high up in its dark perch,

Up there in the insidious shadows,

Awaiting another human meal at noontide.

**DIGESTED BY THE DUST**

So, what happiness did I find in my 73 years?

Years that seemed to fly by like a hummingbird in April.

I found ineffable joy

In the phenomenal nativity of my twin boys.

Found indescribable ecstasy

In the tender embrace of my loving husband,

Found incomparable elation

In the survival of my children and grandchildren.

Living descendants, you are always welcome to loiter at my grave.

Bring a pack of cards though.

I am always up for a new ante.

POEM 58

# JAMES MCKEE ROGERS
# 1836–1900

I offer up this epitaph as an ode instead,

An ode of love, affection and gratitude

To Whittier, my true home away from my one true home.

I dedicate this plain and humble song

To finding this paradise in the mustard fields

To finding peace and serenity in these kindly hills here,

Hills shaded by a thousand trees

In truth, trees planted for purposes unstated and unspoken,

Trees used for hiding the human follies and frolics

Of my brothers and sisters in the faith

Acts of hidden intimacies not seen by the eyes of the Quaker elders.

My friends, you cannot imagine the beauty of the sunrise

Here in my beloved Whittier

The erect beauty of one particular sunrise

On a summer's morning in 1889.

I remember Hattie and me riding double in the heights

Scanning the far-away Pacific blue

Scanning the infinite translucence of a million heartbeats.

Down, down the ever-spreading, ever-descending landscape.

Up there in the heights we found a special magic,

Found the crash of cymbals and the bang of a thousand drums!

Found the flight of a thousand eagles and

## DIGESTED BY THE DUST

The stampede of a hundred wild horses!

And so my friends, and

To Whittier, I say adieu!

Adieu and goodbye to a life of repeating days and nights

Of forgotten repeating conversations

With dozens of old friends now dead and gone.

The worms of Clark Cemetery know them all

Know of the hidden intimacies not seen by the living.

They have found propitiation for the sins of mankind.

**POEM 59**

# VIOLA FULLER
# 1879–1909

For it is written in solemn Chinese ideography,

That two women under one roof spells trouble.

For indeed my life found trouble

And death quite early due to influenza.

I spent my leisure hours in China Town

16 miles to the west in old Los Angeles.

Spent hours in the mildewed shops and the seedy cafes.

Finding culture, romance and ruin in the moody moonlight!

Finding spontaneous spasms in the back musty rooms.

It is true Roscoe Settle found my inner source.

He probed for the truth of my deep hidden springs.

Riveting moist springs of passion and sexual majesty.

Together, as like intertwining tied ribbons,

We embraced the spectral fireworks of a multitude of shooting stars!

Embraced the soaring glissandos of life and love!

But in the end

I decided to kill him dead.

I could not bear for one more minute, the other woman,

That other thing named Lottie Gordon.

But it all backfired on me.

For instead, I killed his father,

One Marcus Settle: late of Whittier Town.

**DIGESTED BY THE DUST**

Forgive me Providence, for I have sinned.

But in my sin,

I have found eternal rest from my nagging jealousies.

Found eternal peace from the tortuous kisses

Of one Roscoe Settle!

## POEM 60
# CHRIS RISUM
# 1865–1920

She was the only woman who listened to me.

The only lady who cared enough to care.

For within my own dead marriage

I was sadly alone, pathetically ignored and ridiculed.

For while I was alive, I was an afflicted man.

A man dead inside himself.

A man endlessly looking for absolutely nothing to find.

With clenched fists and thrown shoes,

I was the man dodging the vitriol.

The man who felt absolutely no love

For the last twenty years of his life.

But alas, I met her.

The only woman who ever listened to me.

My lovely Gertrude,

The tall busty eucalyptus tree

On Rideout Way.

And there I would sit in her sensual shade,

On warm Summer afternoons with my thoughts and desires.

And with the presumptuous winds

Streaming and knifing from the west

She would reach down with her long leafy flowing arms

And allow me,

**DIGESTED BY THE DUST**

A mere man worth absolutely nothing,

To touch her.

To feel incontrovertibly,

Her scintillating life force!

POEM 61
# LEAH SEE
# 1817–1897

I lived 80 long years.

Struggling with sickness and deprivation.

Toiling like a slave

In the mad heat of 80 summers

And the bone-numbing cold of 79 winters.

Striving and straining for happiness and earthly fulfillment.

No man or woman, or God even,

Can take away my honest dealings and daily concerns

For the well, the sick and the dying

Of this former fledgling Quaker community.

But know this old Whittier town,

Town of a hundred years hence,

Yes, you, my once adopted home

By the rising hills to the north and to the east.

Know that my anger for you holds no bounds.

After sweet Artilissa passed away,

You let my grave go to waste.

My tombstone was vandalized and left toppled

By the youthful foolish ones

From the big high school to the south.

Left crumpled and broken

There in the weeds and the trash.

## DIGESTED BY THE DUST

My 80 years as a struggling woman and wife

Left as refuse for the rats!

My final resting place here in Clark Cemetery

Is not to be found now.

You in your temporary wisdom took my name away,

Took my life dates, carved with condoling care,

My allotted years as a breathing thinking human being,

Carved for all time on my beautiful expensive tombstone.

But you took it away in a trash truck.

Mine and my fellow citizens'

Here in this hollowed ground of seeping death.

So, if you dare,

Living ones of the now and the future

Come visit me here in the night.

Come to this haunted old graveyard on Broadway Street.

And I will show myself to you in my anger!

I will show you my living spirit

In all its resplendent colors of the rainbow!

Come boldly, distant cousins and ancestors,

And I will prove to you

There is no death!

**POEM 62**
# IRVEE S. HADLEY
# 1845–1905

Unlike my grounded friends in this venerable bone yard,

Those who lived in this community during its formative times,

Remember where I, Irvee S. Hadley, was finally laid to rest.

For it was my stately ascending tombstone

With the name "Hadley" carved on it

That the bereaved of a thousand funerals

First saw to the left there,

As they tearfully entered into the central avenue

Of the dozen desert palms

Here in Artilissa Dorland Clark's forlorn cemetery.

And when passersby trod with cane and dreadful footsteps

By the southern padlocked gate on Broadway Street

During all those ensuing decades hence,

It was my tall corroding monument they saw

Rising into the sunlight like a spire

Rising from the hardened dirt like an arrowhead

Unearthed by a sweaty mattock.

Rising up like the shank of a giant fishhook

From the dark depths of God's swirling sea.

In short, my life's business was

The planting and the harvesting of citrus trees.

And in truth, my life's pleasure was

## DIGESTED BY THE DUST

The daily night's reading of the Holy Scriptures

With Julia, my wife, and the Kincaids,

Our trusted friends in the faith.

And here I presently rest, peacefully and contentedly.

I have no problems now and I have no debts.

But alas, what of the Woodstock girl?

That rambunctious young thing who thought the dead could not hear.

It seems we were odd bedfellows that night

When the moon was full, there in the ebony sky overhead!

But I was six feet down, throbbing in the darkness of death!

And she, the young Woodstock girl, and he,

Were six feet up, throbbing in the revealing lunar light.

But anon, those two actually thought I was indeed dead!

And thus, I must ask:

Does a tree, deep-rooted and thriving, ever truly die?

POEM 63
# JULIA A. HADLEY
# 1849–1902

Barren Sarah. I knew you well.

Nightly I read of your travails

And of your stoic patience.

I honored my husband Irvee

As you honored Abraham

With my silent servitude and respect.

In service to him,

I fulfilled my earthly destiny

To keep his house and to cook his meals.

I opened the door to him every night at six o'clock for 30 years.

I slept with him through the myriad of nights

Surrendering my female universe to him

As did Sarah in their silken tent.

Ever searching the mysteries of divine deliverance.

Of profound and miraculous conception.

But never finding the key to a woman's purpose

Never finding the door to sustained happiness.

Oh, for a working dowsing rod

That I might have found a son or a daughter

Springing forth from the inner Earth

With the cool calming waters of regeneration

And of maternal satisfaction.

But instead, the walls of our bedroom

There on Newlin Street under the chestnut,

Were as barren as you, old Sarah.

Mother of the multitudes! Mother of the chosen ones!

I died on a Thursday; my body aflame with a ferocious fever.

So what do I have left to offer you, my friends,

After 53 years of fruitless harvests?

Nothing.

Nothing but a silent prayer, perhaps a seed,

Here in the Earth,

For all you barren women without hope.

Know that in death, I am truly at one

With all the countless children of the ages!

I submit my breast to you all!

POEM 64
# JOHN WEED
# 1881–1940

"The quality of mercy is not strain'd.
It droppeth as the gentle rain from heaven…"

The Constable arrested me that day in 1898.
He firmly took me by the collar
There on dusty Broadway Street.
Took me on a horse to the Bailey Street jailhouse
And with an absent smile
And stabbing staring green eyes
He solemnly told me the charges.
That I had willfully accosted one Minnie May Thomas
There on dusty Broadway Street
There under the shadows of the corner jacaranda tree
And with malice and evil intent
Raped said woman,
Inflicting severe pain
And reprehensible humiliation upon her person.
But let it be known, my friends, both dead and alive,
I did kiss the girl!
But as God is my witness
I did not rape Minnie May Thomas!
Judge Seth Gidley from Iowa,

# DIGESTED BY THE DUST

The balded Justice of the Peace

With his grandmother's ancient Bible at his side,

Had mercy upon my terrified soul

And dropped the nefarious charges.

Dropped them "like a gentle rain

Upon the place beneath."

I was but 16 years old when the claws of the law

Throttled me around the throat!

And thanks to the balded one,

I lived on four more decades in sleepy Whittier…

…The Wright Brothers flight…

…The sinking of the Lusitania…

…Women getting the vote…

…The War to end all wars…

…The Prohibition…

…The Stock Market Crash…

…The Great Depression…

…The Repeal of the 18th Amendment…

…The Rise of Nazi Germany…

…The Rise of barbarism and cruelty…

Never was a person more happy to die!

Oh so deliriously happy to die than me, simple me,

One John Weed

Late of this Quaker parish!

POEM 65
# MINNIE MAY THOMAS
# 1878–1902

I have but one overwhelming question:

What did I do to deserve that?

What sin did I commit

To warrant such harsh punishment?

What divine transgression am I guilty of, pray tell,

To be worthy of such abject humiliation?

No real lady should have to endure

What I had to endure.

No dignified and blood-bought Christian person

Should have to tolerate

What I had to tolerate.

Is there a human being amongst us anywhere on Earth?

Is there a beating- heart woman

Somewhere on this furious globe

Who should receive what I received?

It is unspeakable! It is incomprehensible!

But the man who stole my honor

So forcefully, so rudely, so violently,

Went scott free like a snake from the henhouse.

Escaped the scales of righteous justice

Like a pig from the slaughter house!

Like a rat from the beak of a preying hawk!

## DIGESTED BY THE DUST

I truly never got over that day.

Never lived down the attack

That destroyed my womanly heart and soul.

And now, we both lie here in Clark Cemetery,

Buried and digested by the dust.

Covered over with weeds and forgetful fronds.

Only the old jacaranda tree,

There in the restful shadows of old Broadway Street,

Remembers all too well

What happened that long ago day!

POEM 66
# JEREMIAH CLAY
# 1831–1897

To my friends in the faith:

In life, I often observed the ants.

Great profound lessons can be learned

Within the microcosm

Of their silent movements

And relentless deliberations.

I have seen the sanguinary Argentines

Invade the nests of the weaker ones

Have watched them trespass and kidnap and enslave

The lowly ones,

The vulnerable ones,

The perceived inferior ones.

I have witnessed the regal queen

Taken and murdered by her captors.

I have been appalled and dumbfounded

By their muted acts of savagery and cruelty.

And I have been utterly devastated

By the enforced bondage of the black ones,

The nether ones,

The rejected ones.

Great God in heaven!

Where be thy justice?

**DIGESTED BY THE DUST**

Great Jehovah, my Lord!

Let the last now,

Be the first!

POEM 67
# ESTHER SHUGG
# 1833–1908

A woman's heart forever resides

In the glowing hearth of her humble home.

Come Earth dwellers. Come Earth survivors.

I invite you to my warm and cozy house.

There, on the southwest corner

Of Mar Vista and Pickering Streets.

Venture, if you will, to the little white house

With the lace curtains in the front dormer windows.

Peer, if you will, through those simple curtains

And you will find happiness and priceless joy

Embedded on the paneled papered walls there.

Peek, if you will, through those transparent glass windows

And you will find sadness and hopeless despair

Enmeshed on the slatted wooden floors there.

I married James Shugg in 1855, and

Found rapture on my third finger.

I lost James Shugg in 1882, and

Found heartbreak in his bloodied handkerchief.

Come Earth dwellers. Come Earth survivors.

Come to my little cottage on Pickering Street.

Look to the old open window there, and

You will see James and me, mere ghosts now,

**DIGESTED BY THE DUST**

Waving from within,

Waving with friendly testimony,

To a life of steadfast love

And melancholy loss.

**POEM 68**
# MILTON BROWN
# 1822–1917

I knew C. W. Harvey.

Knew him and liked him.

I lived on the first floor of his Greenleaf Hotel

By Bailey Street.

Lived and thrived on the flowered verandah.

Sipped lemonade and gummed soft bread

In the swank dining room.

Talked and listened into the long afternoons

With the fine folks from Illinois and Iowa.

Most of the time,

I rocked and thought back,

And I remembered fondly

The old times in the trackless wilderness,

Seeking a permanent woman and a permanent home.

I found both with a pair of leather boots, a spade and a torn Bible.

Ye Kings and Princes of the Earth!

And to all the rich and the powerful:

"What doth it profit a man

To gain the whole world

And lose his own soul?"

We are truly nothing.

As nothing as the still wind.

As worthless as the dirt

That presently covers my still bones.

Yes, I knew C.W. Harvey.

Knew him and liked him.

He was the richest man in town when I arrived here.

And yet,

He taught me humility and dignity.

Lessons learned with a kind word

And a daily tip of his derby hat.

And after my passing into the eternal night,

He honored me with a kind eulogy at my burial

Here in Artilissa's flower yard.

My forever resting place

Under these countless stars!

## POEM 69
## JOSIE SETTLE
## 1858–1900

The complex calculus of life

Strained my feminine wits

Beyond the bearable!

I don't miss it one bit!

Life was like swimming upstream against the current

With the rushing flood waters assaulting my face

With no mercy.

Life was like climbing a tall steep mountain

With my tenuous grasp steadily slipping

From the rocks

That held me aloft from hopelessly falling.

Falling deep into the gorge far below.

In short, life was nothing but problems and struggles,

And hard tedious work.

Slaving as a kept woman over on Penn Street

I scrubbed the clothes and the walls.

I scrubbed the floors and the dishes

Much too often,

And I hated every minute of it.

And although I loathed my 42 years of human existence,

I loved my son Roscoe

As much as any devoted mother possibly can!

He was the apple of my eye.

He was a good boy and a fine Christian.

Say what you will about my son.

Speak not your derogatory hypocrisies.

Speak not to me any unkind word

Concerning the true love of my life!

Look to the rising sun in the East

And I will reveal to you

The simple calculus of motherhood:

For it was this:

I resolved to ignore the gossip of the unhappy souls

The wretched souls, the demented souls!

This is my advice to you – descendants of a myriad tomorrows:

Look to the rising sun,

And you will see every mother's son,

Cradled in her arms,

Lost in love,

A brilliant binding love

That is beyond any fathomable understanding.

POEM 70
# FRANK J. PAUL
# 1866–1887

The first I was!

Into the first hole they put me.

Down the lane they carried me that day,

Tearfully singing the first dirge for me –

Frank J. Paul –

The first to be interred on Willit Dorland's property.

Mother and father – Thank you. Thank you.

You both prayed long into the night –

For a fortnight –

Fervently prayed on bended knees with folded hands

For my dubious but full recovery from diphtheria –

Wept and prayed -

Fasted and sang for my afflicted body –

Prayed and pleaded continuously-

As my breath shortened and

My heart slowed to a stop.

Mother and Father – Thank you. Thank you.

Indeed, the first of many I was!

Me – Frank J. Paul!

For I was -

The first sunrise!

The first breath!

**DIGESTED BY THE DUST**

The first smile and

The first embrace!

Nothing left to say, except

The first I was!

POEM 71
# MARY MAGDALENE SHELDON
# 1864–1947

Eighty years is but the blink of an eye.

I was born in Illinois on a cold December morning

During the American Civil War

Between the Union North and the Confederate South.

I died in California on a warm October afternoon

During the baseball World Series

Between the Yankees of New York and the Dodgers of Brooklyn.

I was alive

When the slavery of the Negro was abolished, and

I was alive

When the first black man was allowed to play

on the American diamond.

Such fitting bookends for the life

Of this forgotten Quaker woman from Illinois-

The last to be buried in Artilissa's blooming flower bower.

And so, who were my heroes during all those years?

Let this list be my legacy

For those in need of real American heroes:

Abraham Lincoln

Ulysses Simpson Grant

Thomas Alva Edison

Theodore Roosevelt

George Herman Ruth

Charles Augustus Lindbergh

Henry Louis Gehrig

Franklin Delano Roosevelt

Jack Roosevelt Robinson

I remember it now…

I was on my deathbed

There on Camilla Street under the tall desert palm,

And I heard their distant voices in the other room.

Voices of the brave and the true.

And just before I closed my eyes for the last time,

I heard Jackie say to Abraham:

"Thank you! Thank you!"

And then… I blinked.

POEM 72

# WILLIAM HARRISON HARDY
# 1823–1906

I believe a fair introduction is in order here.

Not that a handshake from me could ever take place anytime soon.

I was Captain Bill Hardy:

Proud Indian fighter!

And celebrated toll road builder!

I was the one who built the big road

From San Bernardino to Prescott Arizona!

And it was I, Captain Bill Hardy,

Who founded old Hardyville in Arizona

On the sandy banks of the cool Colorado.

Back when Lincoln was still warm

And the blood of Gettysburg was still not dry.

Back when the old west was coming alive

With wagon wheels and railroad ties.

Growing as a child would

With intrepid enterprise and such derring-do

The likes of which few eyes have seen since!

I came out west from New York

As Captain of a California-bound wagon train

And found a fortune in gold in Placer County.

But it was in the Arizona Territory where I later

Made my mark, and lost my fortune.

# DIGESTED BY THE DUST

Oh my friends. I found out.

Found out what plain hard work can accomplish

And I learned of its resultant riches.

I found out.

Found out what plain greed and dishonesty can accomplish

And I learned of its resultant poverty.

Alas, I was but a survivor in life,

And that was my final legacy.

My friends, have you ever stared death straight in the face?

Have you ever seen the eyes of a wanton murderer

Only an inch away from your own eyes?

Nothing is more frightening and more sobering than that!

But I, Captain Bill Hardy, at your service please,

Experienced it first-hand that day in the scalding desert sand.

That Indian devil was right there!

His nose next to my nose!

But I got away!

Ran away from that place and lived to tell about it!

My friends, next time you come to Clark Cemetery in Whittier,

Go to the eastern fence by Dorland Street,

At the corner there, you will find my little plot of land.

It is a far cry from having an entire city named after you!

But it is a fine and restful spot.

Come closer and lean down to me.

I wish to extend my firm handshake to you all!

POEM 73
# ROSCOE SETTLE
# 1883–1906

By trade and, I might add,

Romantic disposition,

I was a peerless pruner of Whittier's beautiful trees until 1904.

I was the boy who

Trimmed the tall jacaranda trees on Broadway Street.

And the shorter walnut trees by the Strong Ranch on Howard Street.

And I was that same fella who

Manicured and shaped the fully developed orange trees

on Pickering Street

And the sparsely developed pepper trees on Washington Avenue.

With my trusty tool in hand

I cut back many a young tree in this Quaker town

Chopped, clipped and snipped many a bush, flower

and burgeoning branch.

Yes, many a spreading desert palm and towering pine I conquered

Before filling my suitcase with my past

And departing to Los Angeles to save my very life!

And although I worked hard,

And stole innocent kisses

From the lips of many a female flower in this town,

There was only one sublime rose petal for me.

For she was my one true love.

The one I wanted the most, but could never have.

Artilissa Dorland Clark.

Artilissa, when you lost your husband, Aretas, in 1902

I was there for you.

Remember?

I saw your broken heart

And your downcast inundated eyes,

And although I was but a 19 year old boy at the time

And you were but a mature, wilting fragile flower,

I fell hopelessly in love, madly and uncontrollably in love

With your quiet courage, intense intelligence and silent dignity.

If the truth must be known,

And it is appropriate,

Since I am now quite dead,

I left this town in 1904 because of the death threats.

Can you imagine?

And when I returned in 1906,

I found an accepting and forgiving town.

And I found Artilissa on the front steps of her house that evening.

When my father died from massive internal bleeding

I found promise and hope in a young man's suicide.

I had lost my entire family,

And I was only 23 years old.

I suppose I died long before I died.

But if you, my friend, had lost your entire family like me

Wouldn't you do what I did?

# THE VOICES FROM CLARK CEMETERY

Wouldn't you turn to an act of mad desperation

Simply to escape this paralyzing loss?

Only the coroner and Mr. White knew this, but

I ate arsenic mixed with steamed cabbage for lunch on that last day.

And as I lay dying in agony on shady Penn Street

I remembered faintly the greatest moment of my young life.

It was with Artilissa.

We were sitting on a bench in the cemetery, her cemetery,

Next door to her Queen Ann cottage.

It was evening time, and

A full moon was hovering in the low western sky

beyond the walnut trees,

Just hanging there without strings like a shining silver medallion,

Her head resting upon my shoulder.

Her tears finding comfort and understanding

In the soft crevices of my warm sweater.

"Just remember Artilissa," I recalled saying to her.

"There is always hope in a new full moon."

She looked at me and smiled.

That is all, my friends.

I have said enough here.

Come to Clark Cemetery on an October evening sometime.

Sometime when the moon is full and bright.

Look for me and Artilissa beyond those walnut trees there.

We will be sitting in silence.

# PART TWO

# THE VOICES FROM MT. OLIVE CEMETERY

## POEM 74

## LEANDER SKUMFELDT
## 1864–1916

Truly my friends

Dying was my greatest fear, while alive.

My most dreaded

Most detested of future experiences.

Dying, finally, was my greatest achievement

My greatest joy!

My highest calling!

The summit of my scant human existence!

Old Whittier town,

I have missed you indeed,

Have missed the bumpy rides by wagon and horse to Los Coyotes,

Have missed the starry nights of suave embraces in Sycamore Canyon.

With eyes wide open

I saw the irony of my life,

There, on a long table at Pio Pico.

There, amidst the old pottery and the sombreros

A single pressed morning glory

From the Spanish Bible of The Don,

A single fragile fading flower,

A metaphor for a sad but ecstatic soul,

My somber sullen soaring soul!

Be it known: I lived my life quietly

In the fear of God, and

I died my death screaming curses to his face!

But, truly my friends, truly

I found brazen beauty

Found unimagined enticings

In the final gasping exhalation

Of my last heartbeat.

## POEM 75

## GERTRUDE BANGLE
## 1895–1914

By name I was called Trudy.

When living.

Dear friends of the living,

Do you know Whittier town Is a very haunted town?

Do you know my ghost still walks

Still silently steps by you?

Oblivious you?

Here in the stalking shade of the myrtles?

Here in the dark shadows of the walnuts?

I still seek the solace from a seeping sadness.

Still seek the light of truth

The air of freedom

In a dark smothering hole

Here in Mt. Olive Cemetery.

Come my friends, come to me now.

Come inside this old resting ground

This long deceased land of a thousand yawning holes

And find my wandering ghost.

You will find me lurking by the Bailey and the Baird graves

Here in the dark belly of death and life eternal.

Here in the stalking shade of the myrtles.

DIGESTED BY THE DUST

POEM 76
# JOHNNY W. BARROW
# 1890–1914

I was appalled!

Appalled and flabbergasted indeed!

Indeed, when I heard in 1912,

Heard that which I did not comprehend

Heard that which was absolutely impossible

Heard that which was absolutely improbable!

I wept, wept as Christ wept,

That night in April, long ago,

In the dark gray garden under the olives there,

Under the silent screaming stars there,

That night in April

When the invincible, the seemingly unsinkable happened.

I too was like him.

The whole world was my oyster!

The universe was at my calm command!

Nothing could destroy me!

Nothing could defeat me!

Nothing could slow me down!

Then, as with that impossible sinking,

That impossible undoing,

I too descended to the dark depths

Here in Mt. Olive Cemetery.

Not even the ice bags bestowed upon my chest

Not even the desperate prayers

Said in faithful earnest on my behalf

Could reduce the flaming fiery fever

That incinerated my heart, mind and soul.

# DIGESTED BY THE DUST

**POEM 77**

# OLIVE RABEDEW
# 1895–1911

Trudy and I both knew

Both knew and experienced

The voracious vertigo of secret love.

Homework was done together

In the soft lamplight

Of crisp autumn nights.

Plaid ginghams were sewn together

In the wilting afternoon sunlight

Of long forgotten summer days.

Hand-held strolls were surreptitiously taken

In the forbidden fields, and

In the concealed canyons.

Pursed caresses were exchanged

In the innocent dooryards, and

In the curious kitchens

Behind closed oaken doors.

But our Lord decreed in 1911

That our love would desist.

That our intense times together

Would terminate for eternity.

Trudy dearest, let it be known now:

True love is a blossoming tree

## THE VOICES FROM MT. OLIVE CEMETERY

Which yields many kinds of fruit.

Our harvest together then,

Is our legacy, Our last

And final stand for freedom.

POEM 78
# NELLIE B. CHANDLER
# 1897–1911

There I am.

Here I am now.

I am the six year old girl

Behind the glass window

That wide open wedge to the north

From inside my classroom there

At Evergreen school, 'neath

The towering ascending elm trees there,

Shrouded in immense shade.

I am standing and staring there

Daydreaming and yearning and desiring

For my mama and papa

To come get me here,

Wishing and waiting, waiting and hoping

For them to come get me and take me home.

I hate it here!

I hate school!

My forward gaze to the north

Extends out forever as the moon

Stretches its beams, outward outward, and beyond

The limitless fantastic scenes in black space.

I see out there to the north

## THE VOICES FROM MT. OLIVE CEMETERY

I see four faces in the distance there,

Friendly faces, familiar faces

Of family and friends, all

Now asleep with me here,

Here in the cool calm tombs

Of Mt. Olive Cemetery.

There I am.

Here I am now.

Mama. Papa. Come get me!

I hate it here!

I am waiting...waiting...waiting...

Shrouded in immense shade.

POEM 79
# DAVID MORRIS
# 1840–1914

I was indeed a rich man!

A lucky man, a family man,

A man firmly ensconced in the faith

Of the Nazarene.

It is written my friends

That to live for Christ

Is the summit of wisdom,

For wise men still seek Him!

And to die for Christ

Is the absolute acme of human existence.

Rachel and I came to this heaven on earth

When the roads here were dirt in the summer

And mud in the winter.

Yes, me and the missus,

My lovely bride and me,

Found a home here in 1894

A comfortable curtained home on shady Milton Street

When the unburdened trees

Of ten thousand acres

Contained a myriad of feathered fledglings.

And so, with our own five chirping sparrows in the nest

The missus and me, we marveled at

Their gregarious growth and

Their high intrepid flight!

To the northern icy regions

Our first fragile sparrow flew.

Lizzie, my fledgling wanderlust,

Found simple salvation in a cold wooden Iowan pew.

And later, found everlasting life and love

On the frozen Arctic tundra

Of ten thousand luminescent northern lights.

As far north as Dearing Station, my friends,

Twenty miles from the Arctic Circle

Our Lizzie travelled,

Travelled with steadfast faith,

A faith so firm, so unyielding,

It put me, her proud and faithful father,

To shame.

## DIGESTED BY THE DUST

POEM 80

# ANNE SIMPSON SCOTT
# 1895–1932

Friends, my friends,

I do remember.

On the night before leaving to France in 1917

George held my hand.

He held it firmly in his perspiring palm,

Held it and would not relinquish

His gallant grasp. I recall too,

He, taking his left loving index finger

And smoothly, affectionately, precisely,

Stroking my left accepting index finger

Like a soothing balm, like a healing descending brook

As it lapps and caresses the shivering earth

In the silent tranquil evenings of renewed Spring.

## THE VOICES FROM MT. OLIVE CEMETERY

Friends, my friends

I do remember.

On our wedding day in 1921

George held my hand.

He held it firmly in his perspiring palm,

Held it and would not let go.

Not even for five fateful forgotten minutes.

Friends, dear friends,

I do remember.

On the morning I died in 1932

George held my hand.

He held it gently, reassuringly, resignedly

In his trembling perspiring palm,

Held it quietly, bravely, sadly

And would not let go.

And now friends, we are together again

Here in this deep sleeping earth

This dreaming drowsy earth

Here in Mt. Olive Cemetery

He on top of me

Our skeletal long fingered hands

Enjoined, enmeshed and entwined

Forever in the dust

Forever in the dark blooms of death.

Oh friends, my friends

I do remember.

## POEM 81
# DENNIS CUMMINGS
# 1844–1920

To my friends of the 41st Infantry!

My men, my brave brothers from Wisconsin, are invited!

Invited RSVP to my domesticated, but dignified digs

On South Milton Street in Whittier town,

There, above the tracks of the Southern Pacific

There, surrounded by my better half's tulips and pumpkins

There, surrounded by unequivocal respect and love

Of my loyal and nagging better half, Ellen, and

Of my dutiful and loyal son, Lee Roy.

There is a window upstairs facing north,

North to the rising green hills of Whittier town,

North even to the Stars and Stripes

Of my Wisconsin brothers

Of my fellow Wisconsin freedom fighters!

Nightly there, I light a candle for my friends.

My intrepid men, my brave brothers!

Those charging advancing storming souls

Those rampaging, death-staring warriors of the 41st!

Like the fiercely flowing rapids of the Tennessee

There in Chattanooga, and thereabouts,

My brothers and my friends braved the bullets,

Faced the fusillade of fire, the unspeakable violence, and

Even found glorious sacrifice,

Found glorious death in battle,

In the suffocating smoke and sulfur

Of fifty thousand muskets.

Yes, you are invited my brothers! My friends!

Come to my humble home here on South Milton Street

And look to the upstairs window.

There is a candle burning there for you.

Burning with respectful gratitude.

Burning with a proud silence

For my brave brothers,

The storming rampaging men of the 41st.

## POEM 82
## GEORGIA BROWN
## 1898–1914

We were the deathless dream dancers

The crazy girls with secrets and surprises!

Me and Nellie and Trudy and Olive.

We waited monthly for the full midnight moon

Waited with no words uttered

Our secret times together,

Times and moments never mentioned or known about,

By everyone we knew and did not know,

Except by us, the crazy girls

The deathless dream dancers, barefoot

With satin ribbons in our braids,

We joined smooth perfumed hands and fingers

In old Clark Cemetery

Across Citrus Road over there,

As our sleepy snoozing town dreamed unawares,

And we danced silently, gracefully, freely,

As with the monarchs and the tiger swallowtails

Fluttering in the summer sunlight of our audacious youth,

Our sheer cotton dresses,

Lifting them up, and letting them fall,

Again and again and again,

From the Hadley tombstone, and

## THE VOICES FROM MT. OLIVE CEMETERY

Around the standing procession of desert palm trees

Around and around and around,

All the way over to the Hardy gravestone,

Me and the crazy girls!

We, the deathless dream dancers,

Keepers of secrets and surprises,

Saw something in the moon shadows there,

Something no one else has ever seen!

Yes, we saw the smile of Sappho

Carved with the knife of God

On the stone sepulcher of Roscoe Settle!

DIGESTED BY THE DUST

POEM 83
# HARRY BOATMAN
# 1879–1916

It is true my friends.

A man thinks of many things

While on his deathbed.

A man remembers and reflects and responds.

He responds, as with a child, to

The insistent pleadings and proddings of the wall clock,

Responds and obeys, as with a woman expecting, to

The cosmic commands of the moody evening tides.

The incredible colossal circling globe, of

Spasm and sequence, of eyes opening and shutting.

And there it was my friends!

My last orgasmic breath!

My final desperate inhalation!

My final impeccable embrace!

And when it happened,

When my closing eyes saw sable night at noon time,

Two black and yellow butterflies,

Mating mindlessly in the side garden,

Took me by spirit

High above the wanton walnut trees here,

And at last, I saw

The soft benevolent eyes of sweet Jesus

## THE VOICES FROM MT. OLIVE CEMETERY

Beckoning me to join him, there!

From the blinding masticating center

Of the rising resplendent sun.

## POEM 84
# ESTELLA MURRAY
# 1891–1912

Johnny's was the last face

I saw that April afternoon in 1912.

I admit I was mean to him,

As mean as a starving she-dog in heat.

It's not that I did not appreciate

The blooming rosebud he presented to me

Six months before my untimely demise.

But that thorn hidden beneath it,

Could it not have been removed beforehand?

It's not that I did not appreciate

The long-winded love letter he delivered to me

Three months before my untimely demise.

But that last line written so sloppily, – "I love thee!"-

Could it not have been rewritten neater

And the word "thee" replaced with the word "you?"

It's not that I did not appreciate

The inert standing vigil he kept for me

Three days before my untimely demise.

But what was that fool doing out there?

Just standing in the garden out front-

Outside my open-curtained window?

Could he not at least have stepped to my front door

## THE VOICES FROM MT. OLIVE CEMETERY

There on Friends Street

And cried real tears for my departing soul?

But no! That fool, Johnny Barrow,

Instead stood out there flirting with his new girl-

Insipid April and her moody mornings and afternoons-

Standing and staring straight ahead

Like some stupid stone cold statue!

"Oh happy dagger!" the young Juliet once intoned.

"Oh happy death!" I said at last,

There on my mother's divan,

Forgetting once and for all,

That staring unmoving fool, Johnny Barrow!

DIGESTED BY THE DUST

POEM 85
# DEWEY HICKS
# 1900–1918

It burns, burns still.

This sweating insidious fever.

This slippery revolting slide

Down down down into the hole here!

I'm on fire mom! More ice!

Strawberries, sweet strawberries!

Please, please something sweet, something

Something cold, some ice

Yes, ice for my parched tongue!

I can still taste!

I can still hear!

But, but I can't see.

Dear God, where are you?

Dear mother, I need you now!

Please, please, some ice for my lips, my flaming tongue!

It burns! Burns!

Sunset screaming, screaming!

My voice yelling hurling invectives!

My glove, my hat, my ring,

And over there by the door

Her sweet sweet photograph in a glass frame!

Strawberries! Sweet strawberries!

# THE VOICES FROM MT. OLIVE CEMETERY

Please please my tongue is scorched!

Down down down into the hole here.

It burns, burns still.

## DIGESTED BY THE DUST

POEM 86
# LUELLA MAY POLAND
# 1907–1922

The ocean sings my sad refrain.

Sings as the lapsing afternoon

Turns to twinkling twilight.

It sings the polyphonic notes and harmonies

Of a life at once wondrous and magical

And then tragic.

The soft but harsh music of ebb and flow

Of loving, living and then, simply dying.

It sings masterfully the pleasing chords

Of desire and curiosity and fantasy.

It sings the distant aloof music

Of forgotten memories in the gloaming sundown,

Of lost minutes in the stunning shadows,

With the only boy I ever kissed,

The only boy whose trembling touch I allowed

Upon the small of my back,

There in the caressing shade of infinite arousal,

There in the absconding darkness of thrilling intimacy!

Indeed, the ocean sings my sad refrain.

It sings now and forever.

It sings the soft music of the stars.

The magical wondrous harmonies

# THE VOICES FROM MT. OLIVE CEMETERY

Of ebb and flow,

Of wind and time and space.

It is finished.

# DIGESTED BY THE DUST

POEM 87

# JOHN MOLINA
# 1905–1923

Luella Poland – That name!

That face! Those eyes!

Those long lovely locks of chestnut brown!

Those smiling puckered lips in the dizzy afternoon!

Luella! I love you! I need you!

Alas, I do not feel your arrested heartbeat.

Your electric probing touch.

But alas, I do feel your undulating soul.

Your hard penetrating stare.

From over there!

In the smothering weeds.

From over there!

By the David Morris grave.

Luella! I love you! I need you!

And so, when I saw him kiss you that day,

Over there!

By the front rusted gate,

Over there!

Amidst the lilacs and the hushed screams,

I died a hundred deaths.

And, I descended dreadfully to the land

Of dry sleep.

Descended downward to the kingdom

Of stilled atoms.

Of unspoken testimonies,

Testimonies of reaching, ever reaching, and

Never retrieving.

My soul now is bathed in tears.

Tears I shed for thee, my dearest Luella.

Oh, that name!

That face! Those eyes!

Luella! Luella!

I love you! I need you!

**DIGESTED BY THE DUST**

POEM 88

# GENEVIEVE STODDARD
# 1892–1912

Whose footsteps do I hear

Up there above my sleeping bones?

Whose unghostly shadow stalks me

Here in these dark parameters?

Whose blood stream has inundated me

Here in these forbidden avenues?

Avenues of green and gray and alabaster?

Is that you Trudy dear?

Up there frolicking with the night rats?

Dancing with the barn owls?

Oh I remember him well indeed.

The picture of the perfect boy

Stamped inside my dead brain.

Stamped like a frozen prayer at Sabbath time,

Unheard and unanswered.

A splendid boy for whom I pined.

Roscoe my love,

I was too young to taste your eyes.

Those big blue orbs from the skull of Apollo himself.

So, in homage to you, my love,

I was the silent witness of them,

The ladies of the full moon

## THE VOICES FROM MT. OLIVE CEMETERY

Skipping and jumping

Swooning and spasming,

By your huge imposing white stone,

There amidst the night rats,

There amongst the barn owls.

## POEM 89

# ORVILLE C. CAMERON
# 1889–1914

Oh, such larks indeed.

Over at the State School pond,

Way back in the tuft of Eucalyptus shade,

We swam, we yelled, and we laughed.

We, the gang from lower Painter Street,

We, the tough boys with fists of brass!

We heckled, we jumped and we cursed,

The big boys from upper Newlin Street,

Those cowards with flowers for fists.

Ha! They thought we couldn't stand.

They thought we would run and hide,

Here in this Dorland bone yard.

But we stood our ground that day,

That donnybrook day in 1905,

Way back, way back in the tuft of cypress shade,

Over by County Road and Hadley Street.

We boys, the tough boys, with kicks of iron! Stabs of steel!

Our finest moment while alive,

My finest memory while dead.

So, how did I die you ask?

Sorry, but no response from me.

Just ask the Big Boys from upper Newlin Street,

Those cowards with flowers for fists.

## POEM 90

# DAISY MAY BROWN
# 1891–1913

Minute by minute

I crawl on air, and

I crawl in the dirt amidst the worms,

Bracing myself strongly,

Waiting for the eternal dare.

Step forward dying one

And listen to me, the dead one.

Step forward blind dying ones,

And kindly give me your eyes.

I slink back here in my dusty grave,

I ooze silently here in the blind gaze of Tiresias,

Father Time with no voice or tongue.

Minute by minute,

My breathing soul rides the hard earth,

Like naked Poseidon with trident for teeth.

I did not have to die so young!

My friends, you can close your book,

But never close your mind.

My friends, you can close your door and lock it,

But never close your heart.

Frankly, I found life to be a perplexing puzzle,

A puzzle for the confounded and the confused,

## DIGESTED BY THE DUST

A maze for the noble lost.

Minute by minute I rot,

Fodder for the walnut trees here,

Masticating monsters with fear for teeth.

I crawl in the dirt here amidst the worms,

I wait here, waiting for the eternal dare.

POEM 91

## MABEL VERA CONE
## 1893–1911

No one knew I existed.

No one knew I died.

No one, not even my family,

Knew I lived in the back,

Out back, way behind the small white house

On shady Canobie Street.

No one cared one iota.

No one wondered where I was

Or where I was going.

If loneliness were a flower,

I would be the faded one,

Growing and struggling reluctantly

Amidst the devouring weeds,

Out back, way beyond and hidden there,

Amidst the consuming burdock

And the golden creeping jenny there.

When I died that day,

The last Saturday in moody June,

I was alone and afraid.

No one knew I existed.

No one, not even my family,

Knew I was dying.

## DIGESTED BY THE DUST

Dying in the darkness,

Dying of inescapable isolation,

The disease of misery and melancholia,

Out back, way beyond and hidden there,

Behind the small white house,

On shady Canobie Street.

POEM 92
# NOBLE RENNAKER
# 1885–1911

Indeed! Ask the dead and they will tell!

They will reveal what true beauty is.

They will tell us the secrets of forgotten Eleusis.

Indeed! I know how Romeo,

Of fair Verona's Montagues,

Must have felt, when he too,

Experienced the resounding joy

Of love at first sight,

But that sight, let it be known,

Only I knew of,

Only my eyes saw the connection,

And I spied and peeked and peered,

Unknown in the shadows,

At my oblivious mistress in purple,

My dream lady, my love.

Watching as a soldier at guard watches,

Watching for movements in the distance,

Listening for sounds, whispers, giggles,

Peeping at naked shapes,

And bending silhouetted turns.

And with pleasing moans and gaspings,

From behind the closed back doors,

Doors draped in concealing green garlands,

I saw her hair cascading in the shadows,

I heard her muted voice reaching for something soothing.

I watched her my friends!

Watched her at all hours of God's day!

Peeped and peered and spied,

Watched silently there,

Saw wonderful visions there,

Her sorrowful breathings.

She, my love,

Soaking in scented baths of oil

In the soft candlelight there

Way out in the back at dusk,

Over on old Canobie Street.

## POEM 93
## FRED KING
## 1915 (ONE MONTH)

Welcome to Mt. Olive.

Come inside.

Don't be afraid of us ghosts.

Now come down the southern lane,

Keep going past the dense walnut trees,

Past the Morris and Bangle graves,

On to the far left corner,

Hidden by the manzanitas and the monkey flowers there;

See the cracked slabs of cement in the gloom?

See the names of the dead babies scrawled there?

Scrawled with a rusty trowel.

This is the Potter's Field.

This is the grave of the dead babies.

This is the island of the fragile candles

That never felt the flames of life and love.

Genuflect to us, the dead babies!

And bow down to your God!

I know nothing of your earth,

But I do know

It is a fearful thing,

To fall into the hands,

Of a living God.

## DIGESTED BY THE DUST

POEM 94

# PEARLEY KIRKLAND
# 1901–1914

Riding double one day

In musty Sycamore Canyon

With Dewey Hicks on "Belle,"

His old cranky mare,

We watched the stubborn ascension

Of the sultry sun,

Through the cloak of sycamores and willows there,

And transmitted from his mouth

To my naive ears,

I heard the wisdom of the ages!

Heard the voice of tenacious truth

And rigid reality.

He told me I was in need of a savior.

He told me of the Nazarene, magnificent;

The Alpha and the Omega, everlasting;

The Eternal Redeemer, superb;

He told me of the Rose of Sharon, sublime.

Dewey took my hand that day,

That warm and wonderful day,

And I accepted the spectacle at Golgotha,

Accepted the screaming cry of the Skull.

And then, with blustery April, my time arrived.

## THE VOICES FROM MT. OLIVE CEMETERY

I died of influenza, with

Dewey reading the twenty third psalm.

When I breathed one last time,

I closed my burning eyes, and

Saw the Rose of Sharon, sublime.

## POEM 95
# JACOB LUETWEILER
# 1865–1948

From Highland Illinois I travelled,

Travelled with wife, children and the family bible,

Came with stout brethren and brothers in the faith.

And my far-flung epitaph is this:

My friends, I have seen the rain!

I have held the rain in my cupped calloused hands,

Heard the rain as it descended like a demon!

Assaulting the dry land without mercy,

Annihilating the barren and dead land,

As it washes and whirls,

Whispers, envelops and quietly caresses.

My friends, I have stood in the rain!

Stood in the inundations at Beaumont,

Stood sentry and expectantly there,

In its merciful, cleansing invocations,

Stood watching the approaching rain,

Come to earth like dead children,

Come from heaven,

Come to bring drink to the thirsty valley,

Come to bring hope for the new harvest.

My friends, I have seen the rain!

Felt the rain as it purifies and slakes,

Baptizes and consecrates;

Seen the rain from my gaping window

Many times in old Beaumont,

Inside the white house by the river there,

With Fannie, my brood, and a murder of crows.

My friends, indeed, I have seen the rain!

Come to earth like dead children,

Come from heaven.

## POEM 96

# FREDERICK WADDELL
# 1893–1919

Kathrene Mary cojoled me not to blush.

Blush as red as a boiled lobster.

Kathrene Mary insisted that I not touch.

Touch and grope as a feathered Jove.

In the eternal equinox of April evening,

She gave me a signet ring,

With my initial engraved thereto,

As a token of our tryst together.

"W" reminded me of her,

Her voluptuous facade,

Her voluminous assemblage,

Her robust vanguard,

Of desirous daydreams in the suave shadows,

Of amazing nocturnal delights,

Of lickerish ravishments and

Private investigations,

In the astonishing membranes

Of abject titillation.

But let it be known:

I died devastated,

Devastated that I never beheld

My sweet son and daughter,

## THE VOICES FROM MT. OLIVE CEMETERY

Devastated that I never beheld

The sagging bosom of old age.

And now here in my grave,

I blush for the worms.

POEM 97
# KATHRENE WADDELL
# 1899–1921

Truth be known,

I married my man too young.

Truth be known,

I jumped into the warm waters of mad love,

Not able to navigate its crazy rushing currents.

I sought to understand the pangs of passion,

The wantonness of a grown woman,

While but a girl still.

"Wisely and slow. They stumble that run fast."

Truth be known,

I passionately loved and loathed my man,

But then he died and I found another...

Another soothing caressing fondling man,

Shhh!

Dour Mr White,

Dour undertaker man in black suit,

He who found my inherent pulchritude

On the embalming table there,

Downstairs in the chemical darkness of repeating death,

He who found my singing soul,

My sunken yearning unseeing eyes,

My cold gray kissless lips,

## THE VOICES FROM MT. OLIVE CEMETERY

There amidst the formaldehyde bottles, and
The wilting scented daydream tulips.
And oh, the way he brushed my hair!
So tenderly, so lovingly!

## POEM 98
# ELTON PORTER
# 1907–1924
### (AN ODE TO LUELLA AND JOHN)

My best friend John Molina, and I

Spent many a carefree afternoon on bareback,

Astride the furious gallups

Of our sure-footed steeds;

Barefooted in summer and bundled up in winter;

We rode and ranged over the northern foothills,

Ablaze with mustard blooms in spring,

In search of squirrels and sunsets.

We roamed and roved like Crusaders,

Over those imposing heights,

Awash in winter mud and debris,

Seeking the Holy Chalace of freedom,

But still rich in grace,

Rich in impetuous youth.

And we both talked at length,

About Luella, the girl we most admired;

Certainly not for her obvious beauty, no.

Certainly not for her alluring bashful ways, no.

But instead, for her sublime singing voice.

Ah, I remember it well!

That day in this cemetery long ago,

She sang "All Or Nothing At All" by the front gate there,
And lo, the Muses all gathered in spirit roundabout,
Gathered to christen our surging hearts to the gods,
With a soft embrace,
And a simple kiss.

DIGESTED BY THE DUST

POEM 99

# LOUISE MYERS
# 1896–1917

They shot the Archduke,

And my eyes closed in disbelief;

They sank the Lusitania,

And my heart palpitated.

My friend, this world reels and tumbles and faints,

Lost in endless crises and disasters;

Aghast at the senseless violence and mayhem.

The War To End War commenced,

As I terminated this futile existence,

With a loud curse and a silent prayer;

This leaping lunge into the death ditch!

Once, I secretly applied lipstick,

Unbeknownst to my firm-minded father,

And joyously kissed myself in the mirror.

Oh Narcissus,

Be my lover now!

For the world reels and stumbles and disintegrates,

And I have made this last leaping lunge,

This hysterical thoughtless leaping lunge,

Down, down into the deep death ditch!

## POEM 100
## EMMA RIESGO
## 1897–1919

Alas, I was just a simple soul.

Born second in the corner house,

Over on old Washington Street,

Just a short stroll,

From the college there,

My mother labored for 9 hours

In the sweating shadows,

Upstairs there,

In my dead grandmother's bed,

And out I slunk wet and slippery,

Gasping but not suffocating.

When Mr White brought me here,

My, but the ride was bumpy!

Up Greenleaf Avenue I rode,

In Mr. White's old horse-drawn hearse,

Past the Carnegie Library,

And all those stones there,

Past the Greenleaf Hotel,

And its broad veranda there,

Then left the hearse tentatively turned,

Onto flowery old Broadway Street,

Past the double-towered school there,

## DIGESTED BY THE DUST

On pleasant Pickering Street,

Past the fences and the dusty walls,

Past the granite tombstones

Of this bleak locale.

My friends, life was just a blink of the eye for me.

Just a simple soul,

Who found love at last,

In the cold dusty embrace

Of these old walnut trees here.

## POEM 101
# GEORGE SCHULTZ
# 1898-1917

I was reposing voiceless on my deathbed,

As with the silent fog on a winter's morning,

On the way out of here from kidney failure,

And as I closed my windows there,

On north Painter Street,

I tried to recall the greatest day of my life.

In pain, I remember grimacing there,

And then, ten minutes before my heart said "no,"

To this sad comedy called "Existence,"

I saw inside my fading mind

That still moment in time,

That priceless artifact of mere memory:

I saw Georgia Brown and me,

Embracing and shivering like two birds at sunrise,

Holding on to each other in the December drizzle,

Of a long-forgotten morning in 1913,

By the tall flagpole at the high school,

There on busy Philadelphia Street.

And even though I knew her heart,

A loving heart which belonged to another, and another,

She still accepted my romantic entreaties;

My hushed whispering words of sweet infatuation;

## DIGESTED BY THE DUST

And that, my friends,

Is what I miss the most:

The fragrant audacious flirtations,

The deeply passionate naïveté,

Of the one and only Georgia Brown!

## POEM 102
## LOLA STANLEY
## 1913–1918

This side of the veil,

No living human has ever seen,

No mere mortal has ever beheld,

The diamond stutted rainbow face,

Of the One, Iam

With streams of flame,

Flowing from the Axis,

His all-seeing eyes,

Can be felt like crashing waves,

Of silent sound, silent...

Like rushing ripples of watery light,

The Eternal Seed,

The everlasting bloom;

Of the One, Iam

The only flower, silent...

There is no softness of sleep here,

No mark of darkness or sweeping escape,

We spirits of the Eternal Seed, instead

Fly as the dandelion blooms fly, silent...

Weightless, floating and drifting,

Seizing the morning shade of timelessness,

A multitude of soaring souls,

**DIGESTED BY THE DUST**

A single speck of mercy;

No. You have not seen what I see.

Now and forever-

His magnificent being embraces me,

As a silvery swan

Embraces a goddess!

POEM 103
# JOE LICON
# 1904–1920

Who was that coughing at my side?

Which of my manly pallbearers

Leaned upon my casket

On that distant funeral day?

Who was it that yawned,

Loudly, sleepily, lazily,

On the day they covered my bones with dry dirt,

Here in the comfortable darkness,

Of shadowy Mt. Olive Cemetery?

Who was it that said: "I will miss him,"

Even when he began tapping his restless fingers,

One after the other,

Upon the wonderful mohogany finish,

Of my well-made polished coffin?

To whom do I credit for

The distilled drops of sated tears,

Which fell noisily upon the buttercups,

Dotting my newly-made grave?

My friends, don't ever imagine that we,

The dead are dead,

When you, the living, bury us.

For we can hear your plaintive cries of "O," moaning;

We can feel your grieving hearts, breaking;

We can taste your "tempest-tossed" tears, slaking.

So, my friends,

Who was that coughing at my side?

Kindly lend him a handkerchief, if you please.

POEM 104
# GRACE THOMPSON
# 1894–1917

At the timbered railroad depot,

On lower Philadelphia Street,

Across from the lumber yard and the state school there,

I spent many an erstwhile afternoon,

Sitting and worrying and waiting,

Like an expectant Ceres,

For the returning equinox,

Like an agonizing Penelope,

For her long lost love,

From the ancient shores of Ilium,

Waiting and hoping in the spring rain.

And I thought a thousand thoughts,

About life and love and finally dying.

And I also thought much about my wonderful father,

My gentle fitful father,

A wayward, kind soul he was,

Who, out of the blue,

Left the town and our family behind,

Left to find greener pastures as he said,

And who promised to return,

When his oats had at last been wildly sown.

And I waited and waited,

# DIGESTED BY THE DUST

Praying and hoping,

That the next train would at last bring,

His lovely humble smile,

His relaxed eyes, and handsome hermetic brow.

But my endless patient waiting,

Came to a halt that day in cloudy April,

My last day alive,

When again, the tremulous train arrived,

There at the timbered railroad depot,

Across from the state school and the lumber yard,

And once again, he was not on board.

And so, here I am now,

Still waiting patiently, expectantly,

In my dusty forgotten grave,

Waiting for just a single simple flower,

From the only man I absolutely adored,

To be placed upon my single simple tombstone.

POEM 105
# CARL KOONTZ
# 1892–1915

Mister Gregg was standing atop my grounded skull,

And so was Mister White,

And the reticent county coroner.

And inexplicably,

They directed two men in blue overalls

To dig up my decomposed body that day.

I must say, the sounds of those slicing shovels,

Upending the dirt of my final destination,

Here in Mt. Olive Cemetery

Was most disheartening, to say the least.

But bigger and better digs

Were in store for me,

Up at Whittier Heights Cemetery.

"Easy fellas, easy," I said silently,

"Easy now, as you lift me out!"

And "heave-ho" I heard the men say,

As they hoisted me up upon

The four-wheeled wagon,

With two sturdy horses up front

Looking back dubiously.

And together, with my one ton marble tombstone,

I and my lilly white sarcophagus

## DIGESTED BY THE DUST

Travelled to the Heights,

Whittier's new and spacious boneyard,

Festooned with wild roses.

Though it is impossible to die permanently twice,

I have discovered in death,

That it is possible to be buried a brace of times!

"Heave-Ho" I heard the men say!

POEM 106
# IVEY WALKER
# 1887–1916

Verily, verily, my friends!

You are all dead now.

So I can speak candidly.

I found out,

When my ripe red rose bloom

Opened early, mysteriously,

Wantonly, as with all crazed flowers,

Drunk with the wine of forbidden delights.

I found out,

There is no real meaning in life.

Except in the insatiable passions

Of the hopelessly human heart.

Money. Politics. Education.

Friendships, Status. Travels.

Books read. Culture. Faith.

All these diversions pale in comparison,

To the wanton gazes and gropings

Of erotic desire,

Of euphoric fleshy meshings,

Of excited intense arousals,

Behind and decidedly beneath

The lacy curtains of magical meetings

In the dark!

Verily, verily, my friends!

You are all dead now,

So allow me to ask you,

What is the point of one more step forward in life,

Forward, into the uncertain destined avenues of the future,

If desire and its attendant dances,

Are not experienced and realized?

I was seventeen in 1904,

When my trembling hand found the accosting arm

Of one Roscoe Settle.

Ravished as a rose bloom by thorns,

He guided me here and there,

To the amazing gardens of senses and screams,

And with no regrets or guilt,

I found God that evening,

In the stone temples of tender touches,

And deathless sensations.

Verily, verily, my friends,

I indeed found out

The real meaning of life,

I found it in the sweaty secret embraces,

Of one Roscoe Settle!

POEM 107
# ELMO STRAIN
# 1917 (ONE DAY)

On the cusp

Of deliberate morning,

I saw the mysterious light.

I saw the grace of one day.

It was but a momentary specter.

And I was rich for an hour!

It held me in its warm essences,

It dangled me for one flashing hot day.

One single day of human heartbeats.

Please spare me your sad tales,

Of times wasted and loves lost,

Of missed opportunities and decisions postponed,

Thinking it would never end.

As with you all,

I took for granted

The ticking tryranny of Old Cronus.

It's okay mother.

You can let go now.

No tears.

No tears.

## POEM 108
# FRANK LANE
# 1877–1913

RS was my best friend,

A friend ever to the end.

Together we footed and mounted

The pliant limbs of the Hybrid Tree

On County Road,

And wetfully whistled,

As with birds in the warm zephyrs

Of summer solstice,

At the lassies down below,

With young and perfumed necks naked,

Ready and shivering,

For the ghost dance.

Together we skipped smooth stones,

Upon the staid surfaces

Of the state school pond,

Out back among the chicken coops

And the pig pens;

We howled and hollered,

As with hysterical night beasts,

Wild under the stars!

Together we passed scented posies to Lottie Gordon,

Our intended island of private discovery,

## THE VOICES FROM MT. OLIVE CEMETERY

Our intended treasure,

Our intended Holy Grail!

And with silent tandem ascensions,

There in the enticing moon shadows,

RS and I found a home in the Gordon heights,

Inside the inviting spread-out mansion,

Of a hundred breathless whispers.

## DIGESTED BY THE DUST

POEM 109

# ROSIE ORTIZ
# 1916–1936

The stars are my friends.

They know of my many secrets.

They remember my private musings.

The stars cried tears for me.

They placed fragrant roses upon my bosom.

I sought to comfort them in their grief.

I tried to hold them close in my embraces.

Nightly now, I see them in my gazes.

Midnight now, I hear their muted whimperings.

What can I say to them?

What words of sweet solace can I give?

A single blade of sweet grass understands.

A solitary leaf of autumn knowingly descends;

There is no darkness in death;

There is only love,

And light eternal.

Las estrellas son mis amigas.

Ellos saben de mis muchos secretos.

Recuerdan mis reflexiones personales.

Las estrellas lloraron lágrimas por mí.

Colocaron rosas fragantes sobre mi pecho.

Busqué consolarlos en su dolor.

Traté de mantenerlos cerca de mis abrazos.

De noche, ahora los veo en mis miradas.

A medianoche, escucho sus gemidos apagados.

¿Qué puedo decirles?

¿Qué palabras de dulce consuelo puedo dar?

Una sola hoja de hierba dulce entiende.

Una solitaria hoja de otoño desciende a sabiendas;

No hay oscuridad en la muerte;

Sólo hay amor, Y la luz eterna

DIGESTED BY THE DUST

POEM 110
# CLYDE DURAN
# 1894–1923

Kindly show me the exit sign!

My watch fob is missing.

It is most likely with the trench nails.

Those nails lay strewn by the cat,

Out back amongst the kiln bricks,

And the broken wheelbarrow.

Send for the constable!

Summon the parson with the forked tongue!

Peel the oranges carefully please.

Use the trench nails!

Here kitty kitty kitty.

Have you, my little furry friend,

Seen the exit sign?

Mother may have hidden it, out back,

With the cream cookies.

How dare I once again,

Steal the cream cookies!

Mother Mother.

I tried to please you best I could.

Sorry I displeased you with

My lazy irresponsible ways.

Sorry for being such a disappointment to you.

## THE VOICES FROM MT. OLIVE CEMETERY

Where is my watch fob?

Where is my sweet little kitty?

Send for the constable!

Summon the lying parson!

And kindly show me the exit sign!

DIGESTED BY THE DUST

POEM 111
# ANNA PEARL LONGMAN
# 1900–1916

Dewey Hicks truly loved me.

Loved me as Mark loved Cleo,

Loved me as Pyramus loved Thisbe.

We took many a determined stroll,

With hands entangled delightedly,

Down the cool expectant streets,

Of this quiet Quaker town,

Across the strident fields at noon time,

Seeking a shady spot under the sun.

Happily we found one,

In the still sullen afternoon,

Of my final day on earth,

Way over by the Strong Ranch,

Hidden by the stately pampas plumes,

The ripe strawberry field of the Needham family;

Dewey and me settled in silence that day,

Me feeding him there,

His blond crown upon my brown carriage,

One moist sweet strawberry at a time,

No doubt, our finest moment as lovers.

But then, as with all things in life,

Written and unwritten,

## THE VOICES FROM MT. OLIVE CEMETERY

It ended as my heart stopped,

Stopped as a clock unwound in time,

There in the still summer heat,

Of this quiet Quaker town.

DIGESTED BY THE DUST

POEM 112
# BERNICE MAY
# 1899–1918

Emma and me in 1916,

Spent many a summer Monday morning,

Over there, across Citrus Road,

In old decrepit Clark Cemetery,

Prancing and picnicking amidst

The majestic stone monuments and markers,

Of the redeemed and the damned alike.

Talking and dreaming of later days and years,

Wondering aloud with faraway stares,

Together in our starched skirts

And matching silk stockings,

Of futile futures with men we would never meet.

But oh, the crazy tales we told each other,

Tales of tricks and secrets,

The like of which would put,

The devil himself to blush!

So what is my message to you-

The present alive and the future dead?-

It is this: Seek the unseen.

POEM 113
# WILLIAM SAWDEN
# 1893–1917

On the southern facade,

Of the Golden Rule Store,

On Greenleaf Avenue to the north,

There is a single window,

On the third floor up.

Behind the white half open curtain,

Facing south and southwest,

A sixteen year old boy, once employed there,

Was on his knees facing east.

He was praying earnestly

For a miracle from God.

With words audible and vehement,

Mention was made of a sick father,

A father succumbing to depression and confusion,

To fear and apoplexy.

The father, a man I once respected,

A man I once admired as honest and true,

A good man with a kind disposition; now

Was trapped in the deep pit,

A dark hellish hole,

Of liquid spirits and utter hopelessness.

"Dear God," the boy intoned. "Please,

Please save my father from himself,

Deliver him from

His outraged seething soul."

The boy remained there fifteen minutes,

Praying amidst the wash tubs and the skillets;

And finally, as a drowsy rain

Fell to earth that day,

The boy behind the curtain fell prostrate there,

And cried salty tears of loud desperation,

To augment the afternoon drizzle.

"I am half here and half gone," the boy said.

"Please God, help us!"

And now, as I lie here,

Dead and decayed in the grovelling ground

Of Mt. Olive Cemetery,

I am completely gone,

Gone as the forgotten wind

That once whispered words of hope,

To the quiet lonely ones,

As I was then.

"Thank you God,

My precious redeemer.

Indeed, you heard my words that day,

As I knelt there,

Faithfully facing east.

POEM 114
# BESSIE TRISSELL
# 1891–1914

Alas my friends,

I finally know the truth now,

So here it is, straight out,

The real truth, which resides in a world,

Brimming with insidious lies.

My dear friends, come,

Come to this aged receptacle of the truly alive.

Shh! Sit still, here in the leafy shadows,

And just ponder for a spell,

Disquiet yourselves,

Meditate calmly and know this—

Know that this restful peaceful oasis,

Is the great equalizer indeed,

The great and forbidding bed of death,

Where all sleep in the twilight of time,

Where all must finally come to find eternal rest.

Know too, that here, sleeping motionless,

Under this unsounded sod,

Are the proud and the meek,

The white of face and the black too,

All free now in their moist chilly tombs.

Here too are the rich and the poor alike!

## DIGESTED BY THE DUST

Where I am, your money and gold are worthless,
Worthless as the dirt here,
And your possessions, once owned by you,
Now belong to someone else, who
One day indeed, will be here too,
The once happy and the sad,
Believers in God, and the foolish alike,
The young and the old, the
Powerful and downtrodden,
The brave and the afraid indeed!
All are here now, resting, resting, sleeping.
Stop breathing yourselves now, and sit still.
Sit easy and listen, here
In the wind-disturbed silence,
Of densely dark Mt. Olive Cemetery.
Shh! They are lurking as coy ghosts now,
They sigh in sweet whispers.
They know the truth indeed!
My friends, come join us now,
Come and we will tell thee!
For we are all free now,
Resting, Resting, sleeping
In our moist chilly tombs.

## POEM 115
# BILLY SANDERS
# 1917–1933

Freddie Moore and David Hilberg were brothers to me,

Freddie, a stalwart boy from Hoover Street,

And David, a quiet and congenial lad,

From nearby Dorland Street.

Both fellas were smarter than me,

Both, with muscles on legs and arms,

Ran faster than me.

Both were good with numbers,

But I was good with words.

Truly, I remember that day well,

In 1932, here in Mt. Olive Cemetery,

When Miss Annie from Sydney Mines,

Received the supplications of a grieving earth,

And took up residence in her new grave.

"A Sad day for us all," I heard Reverend Hodson say,

And George Scott, after the service,

Fell prostrate there, inconsolable,

Astride her bed of weeping roses

And wailing chrysanthemums.

Freddie, a true friend I was proud,

To call a friend,

Comforted George, as a compassionate saint would,

With kind hand on the shoulder,

Of a distraught husband in mourning,

"Sorry sir, sorry," I heard Freddie Moore say,

Softly, in the shade of the screaming walnuts.

And when I myself found residence here,

Dead at 16 from influenza,

Freddie Moore, my stalwart friend,

Showed compassion once again,

Putting his caring hand gently,

Upon the sunken slopping shoulder,

Of a crying grieving mother.

"Sorry mam, sorry,"

I heard Freddie Moore say,

Softly, in the shade of the screaming walnuts.

POEM 116

## CARRIE STINNARD
## 1891–1908

No one was supposed to know about it.

No one was privy to what I saw that cloudy day.

That curious and confusing day,

Over there, in Clark Cemetery,

Across bemired Citrus Road,

With the mud puddles and the tire tracks.

Over there amongst the alabaster crosses

And the soaked pliant ferns.

Roscoe Settle and Artilissa Dorland Clark

Were sitting closely together there,

Like man and wife, huddled

At honeymoon in the soft rain,

Her husband Aretas, still warm in his grave,

And she, with her head on Roscoe's shoulder!

Scandalous indeed! Outrageous indeed!

Even here in my grave,

I wonder at that woman's audacity,

Her highfaluting hypocrisy.

I wonder if there were any morals remaining,

There, inside her irrational lustful heart?

At the sight of this – I was indeed,

Scarred for the remainder of my short life!

How could she, an older woman,

Lead that poor boy on like that?

When I died, I died an undefiled virgin girl,

A dedicated servant of the Lord,

A stern and stringent defender of our faith!

Just like him, one Roscoe Settle,

The man of my dreams!

The man whom even God found sinless in His sight!

Amen to the saints of this staggering earth!

## POEM 117
# EMMA RUTLEDGE
# 1876–1914

Greetings my friends,

From this forgotten frump,

This long-dead girl who now haunts

This yawning ghost garden here.

In life, my tongue tasted many terrible lies;

All just worthless words from men,

Men I'd just as soon see dead

While I was alive still.

Just as soon see them buried deep in the dirt,

One after the other,

Here in these fragrant acres of hard silence.

One might think that a smart girl like me,

Might have learned a thing or two,

While breathing still;

Learned that the proffered promises

Of erstwhile cads about town,

Had as much value and reliability

As a sucking sandpit!

But ladies, pray tell my friends,

You know all too well what I speak of!

We all know of their irresistible charms,

And we all know of their universal mendacity!

## DIGESTED BY THE DUST

Even now, damn them all!

"Stay away from me! Stay away!"

But alas, there is some consolation,

Some slight soulful comfort,

Here in this yawning ghost garden;

Here beyond the spiritual membrane:

They are all sleeping now, sleeping

Sleeping as motionless as bears sleep,

Deep, deep in the icy twilight

Of forgotten existence.

POEM 118
# GREEK GEORGE ALLEN
# 1828–1913

Seegh no mee.

Ah, I see we have not been introduced.

Please, if you will, call me George, George Allen.

In life, I was a greek from Smyrna,

Hired by the United States Army,

Long ago when Buchanan was president,

Employed because of my tenacious skill,

Riding atop a grunting dromedary,

Riding and gliding over the great American landscape,

Bringing the supplies for the Butterfield Overland,

Riding day and night most of the time,

From St. Louis to my final home, Los Angeles;

The American Camel Corps we were!

The eight of us: Me, Mico, Long Tom, Short Tom,

And the others, all hard as quartz;

To the virgin western wilderness we went,

Never slowing down our momentous movements,

Or ever looking back in timid fear.

And so, with sweaty craft, and

A satchel full of lucky days,

We completed the route in a year!

And as for the notorious Senor Tiburcio, well,

## DIGESTED BY THE DUST

Do not judge this old skeleton here!

I let him live out back in my stable house;

I minded my own business!

It was either that, or

A single gunshot to my head!

"Eese malaka!"

But I never saw any reward money, I swear,

When the relentless inexorable law

Finally captured and led him to the gallows;

"Pronto."

This dirt here, senor, belongs to you!

Seegh no mee.

I must leave you now,

And find rest in this calming Mexican dirt,

Here in shady Mt. Olive Cemetery.

POEM 119
# SETH S. GIDLEY
# 1832–1916

I will never forget the rain that winter,

And the landslide that still stains my grave.

An evil cursed wind it was,

Lacerating the drenched cliffs

And descending gullies of Rubio Canyon,

With wailing sheets of raining hell!

My friends, as long as this life of ours,

Continues with its temperate turning,

You and I shall never see nor meet any striving soul,

As brave and strong as my delirious,

But loving daughter, Evaline Gidley Drew.

I did indeed find solace in knowing she survived,

That rainy horrible day up by Echo Mountain,

February in '09; no man indeed should have to sit,

Aghast, with the mind-numbing memory

Of one's daughter being buried alive in her own home,

Of one's grandson, missing for the night,

Being found the following morning,

Buried and dead in the debris.

And oh, the bravery of that soul,

Of my Evaline saving her twin girls,

When the rocks and mud began to rumble!

Of my Evaline blindly running into that death house,

## DIGESTED BY THE DUST

When the killing landslide mercilessly hit,
To save her husband and sons still,
Only to be struck down in the descending wreckage,
Barely alive, as it set fifty feet down!
I cannot fathom such courage, my friends.
I am still awestruck, here in my grave.

Praise God they survived that day...
Sans my grandson...Thayer.

Me and Ruth lived seven more years after that,
On shady Milton Street in quiet Whittier.
We lived there through many a fine summer sunset,
And many a fine Yuletide feast.
We grew old in the faith of our Lord,
And died, the both of us, in 1916.
And here we lay by the walnut trees.
But I will never forget that rainy winter,
In Rubio Canyon by Echo Mountain,
Back in '09, near the old Pavilion there,
When Evaline Gidley Drew, my delirious
But loving daughter,
Showed saintly auras that day,
The like of which
You and I have never seen!

## POEM 120
# IDA OAKS
# 1827–1919

John gave me a good home.

Not one with plumbing and power,

But one with a solid slab, and a full well.

And while living in this Quaker homestead,

We found that life was precise and persistent.

But it pleased me to provide good food, and

Medicinal solace for my meager family.

Through those unyielding years we learned

To accept the twists and turns of fate,

And to continue the never-ending bows to prayer.

Death was a returning customer indeed, but

We learned to be silent, stoic and still,

When sovereign Lord Yeshua silently paid a call.

But we had indeed found paradise out west,

Out here in tranquil Whittier town!

Where it never snows at winter,

And the hills here burgeon with wild flowers.

But God was good to us,

And John worked hard to provide a good life for me.

But, Oh! To smell again, just one more time,

The wonderful heavenly fragrances,

Of ten thousand Valencia blossoms,

All crowned with white dancers at springtime!

## POEM 121

# ADA MCDONALD
# 1873–1906

This is a mistake!

A huge contretemps indeed!

A foul up of the most egregious kind!

You see, it wasn't my time yet,

This death thing; I had things to do still.

I had places yet to visit I had never seen before.

I had strangers from distant locales to meet still,

I had a multitude of tomorrows yet,

Or so I thought, having no doubt.

But now, here I am, dead as a doorstop,

At last with all the minions and the predecessors,

At last, all reconciled and made equal.

But you see, I was fine that day.

Thinking nothing tragic would happen to me.

Expecting another evening at home, with

Yet another morning to come, and waking up.

I tell you, I have been wronged!

This is the cruelest of mistakes!

Dear God almighty!

You took away my dream that day!

Robbed me of my perfumed interlude in the shadows,

It was all I ever wanted; just ten groping minutes,

## THE VOICES FROM MT. OLIVE CEMETERY

Naked with my dream lover,

One Roscoe Settle, late of this citrus parish.

But the lights went out, instantly!

Inside my parents old house on North Pickering,

When my brain sprung a leak that day,

And I dropped dead at age 33.

A huge contretemps indeed!

A foul up of the most egregious kind!

# DIGESTED BY THE DUST

POEM 122
# JESSE F. HUNNICUTT
# 1867–1908

They placed me near the gate, there,

My tall tombstone rising above all the others;

All were friends and neighbors way back when,

We worked and worshipped together, in the presence

Of our Lord creator, and savior most wondrous.

They are all dead now, but are alive evermore in his grace.

Step inside this dead world, my friends.

Come closer, over here;

Me and May are soundly sleeping

Here waiting, in the walnut shadows,

Down, way down here, sleeping the dreams of life and love,

Down, way down here...waiting...

Inside this heaping bed of rotting bones,

Dancing gaily in still death, as we once did,

Years ago, alive and alone,

Hidden deeply in the orange fields,

We touched our baptism with water, and fire!

And saw our god in the clouds that day.

POEM 123
# EDNA PURCELL
# 1912–1930

Dying a virgin was the least of my regrets.

Dying a chaste woman at 18 seemed a moot point.

I remember watching my momma die.

It was in summer, and I was 16.

Hopelessly disconsolate, that's how I felt;

How would I live without her?

Why was she so cruelly taken from me?

How did she get so sick?

My demise, then, was the anticlimax of my short sad life.

Oh cruel Fate, you!

I despise your insatiable appetite for shattered lives;

Indeed, I spit on you for all the ill-timings and bad luck.

I spit on your wry smile, lurking there,

Behind the shadowy trellis,

Of private episodes with flowers and silk;

You, with those arrogant knowing glances,

Those imploding muscular arms of private desperation.

I died a virgin indeed, never having you,

Died with an empty heart and a reeling soul.

Life was just a foolish grab for nothing;

Always seeming to have enough,

But always wanting much more.

That was life, my life in this quiet religious town.

So, I died a virgin in 1930. I was 18.

Too late for me, I guess.

All I wanted, was to spit in your face!

Oh cruel Fate, wrecker of dreams!

## POEM 124
# EVERETTE E. HILL
# 1899–1915

Tyrus Cobb of the Tigers.

Honus Wagner of the Pirates.

To simply see those two hit a baseball,
Well, that would have made my last day alive, worth living.
To watch those two run the bases, like crazed jackrabbits,
Well, that would have made my death, worth dying.
To see those two heaving a baseball ninety feet,
Like General Washington pitching that silver dollar like he did,
Well, that would have made my entire life, worth repeating.

"Oh Tyrus and Hons!
American deities indeed!
I call forth your honored spirits in respectful homage!
I summon you both to this invocation of the baseball gods!
Come forth ye warriors of the American Diamond!
Show us please your grip and your glove. Each!
Show us please your stance and your swing. Each!
Kindly know sirs, that we shall relish with fervor,
Your tales of the great games, and the long-ago seasons.
We shall nod in agreement to every word you say! Each!"
Indeed! I remember those two the most, while alive.

**DIGESTED BY THE DUST**

Tyrus Cobb of the Tigers,

Honus Wagner of the Pirates.

## POEM 125
# DELORES MIRELES
# 1907–1923

I gushed forth eight months after his death,

My natural father, a rascal named Roscoe.

My mother, next to me here,

Shall remain unnamed and acquitted,

Even in anonymous death,

For she was not innocent, nor he,

That brazen wolf who found his sniffing way,

Through sneaky vines and groping flowers,

Their brazen squealing passage to mad love,

Of strange probing games in the dark,

With eyelids closed in shuddering tempests.

It was her delirious heart he seized,

And her slithery soul too.

And there, let it be known,

He found an open gaping curtain,

And Dianthus' skin a quivering,

Concealed through a sheer façade of silk,

There, my mother's priceless treasure room,

And in the midst thereof,

Her innermost well of warm moist yearnings,

Her inner sanctum of curious desires,

I emerged on a naked winter's evening,

Shivering in my mother's room of ice.

DIGESTED BY THE DUST

POEM 126

# AMERICA WATTS
# 1851–1934

Mister White buried me here beside Greek George,

Back here, with the wind-tossed weeds and the walnuts.

"Hey George, you old camel driver, you.

Can you hear me over there?

I can relate to your dogged controlling ways."

With invisible trace chains attached to my pigtails,

Mister Watts for 39 years was my master and tormentor;

Five times in our marriage I felt the bloody pangs,

Of his beaded belt, and bare knuckles.

Five times I fled from his house a frighted,

Wondering if I would wake up the next morning alive.

"Hey George, you old camel driver, you,

Can you hear me over there?

I was no beast of burden to beat,

Nor was I his old blanket to hang on the line."

When a possible sixth time erupted in 1891,

I ran to the tool shed next to the privy,

Out back, there, with the lilacs and the bleating ewes.

And I desperately grabbed his bladed axe.

"No Mister Watts! You will not beat me today!"

I screamed, as nearby neighbors looked on.

"No Mister Watts! Never again will I accept this!"

## THE VOICES FROM MT. OLIVE CEMETERY

Looking back on that moment, here in my grave,

I believe Mister Watts was waiting for me to at last resist him.

No more after that was I his silent patsy.

No more was I his old, used-up mare,

His old brow-beaten girl, with ticks, gadfly bites,

And a thousand silent complaints.

"Hey George, you old camel driver, you.

Can you hear me over there?

Truth be known, I stood up to my only love in life."

I finally decided to make a stand against him,

The one who fed, clothed and provided a roof over my head.

And he stopped. He stopped!

Thank the Lord, he stopped beating me!

And here I am, after 83 years of toil, hardship and pain,

Buried happily, way back here,

With the wind-tossed-weeds and the walnuts.

POEM 127
# FRANK GARD
# 1887–1912

I loved her as much as Jesus loves his bride.

My friends, she was my saintly intended, indeed!

Created by my God especially for me; this beautiful flower,

This unmatched star in all the galaxy! She was,

Innocence personified; the apex of all that is holy and good.

Ivey Walker had no sins; she walked with

the magnificent vestal virgins, indeed!

Always alert to the sacred consuming flames within her pure self!

A goddess-like lady of the highest class and caliber; upright and chaste,

Never wont to surrender her graces to me, or any man or mouse!

Even as I proposed, and held her close that night,

Those saintly untouched lips, those wonderful bashful eyes,

Refused to respond to my manful pleadings, and she said no to me.

Shocked and stricken, I stood there and said "Wonderful!"

For I expected this abject denial, this crushing brush off.

Who was I to think I deserved this highest ideal,

This quintessential embodiment of perfect female love?

Not I, indeed. For as a lowly sinner, I confess!

I confess that I secretly desired to find God within her holy tabernacle.

I confess that I secretly wanted to crown her the Queen of Heaven,

With trembling holy fingers, and sweet wine from my manful flask!

But I was not worthy of her! Indeed!

God almighty in heaven!

Damn me to hell for wanting to kiss Ivey Walker's saintly hand!

### DIGESTED BY THE DUST

POEM 128

# IVES MICHAEL RASMUSSEN
# 1892–1919

So, there you are, my friends,

And here I am, resting, nodding off, in the cool dirt,

Of shady and forgotten Mt. Olive Cemetery.

There are many of us here, sleeping, and waiting,

As you are sleeping and waiting, up there,

Above the grass, and the old mossy tombstones.

We all know now what life meant,

We all know now that life was a serious matter indeed.

We all found out that every person must make a choice,

The choice of eternity... here, where we are.

We the dead know now, that life was just a test,

A simple test with an easy answer.

But I am dead now, and so, don't ask me.

The truth must come from him, the Master,

For I am nothing, absolutely nothing,

Just dust and atoms lying askew, here in the dark,

Of shady and forgotten Mt. Olive Cemetery.

So, there you are, my friends,

And here I am, waiting for the final trumpet peal.

Waiting for something no one can possibly imagine,

I am waiting for my savior to open up the big skydoor,

And I am waiting for the tremulous toppling,

Of these old mossy tombstones.

## POEM 129
# CATHERINE BRYAN
# 1838–1918

Thy swan song will be kept short, for thou

And ye, faithful friends of Whittier's Quaker enclave,

In stout shock, thy anger scolds the town,

For ye know, in heart and soul,

Thee and this old maid did not approve or agree,

With ye establishment of said saloon,

And its mad proprietor, with mustache in tow.

To God, in his holy anger, thou sayeth:

Do not spare ye town of Whittier,

Please, kindly show no mercy, as ye sinful township,

Heads into the uncertain evil times,

Cease not to spare the damaging quakes,

From thy emblazoned temper in seasons ahead,

For ye Whittier hath dressed obscenely in clothes of mustard yellow,

And hath exchanged them for the proper, black regalia

of the righteous,

Yes, proper and good accoutrements for thy people in worship!

But now it is time for the old woman to say:

Ye Whittier! Thou hath forsaken the highest God!

For thy immodest music and dancing,

And thy indulgent viewing of sinful cinemas,

In the darkness of Hades itself, at the Optic,

Ye den of corruption and vice,

Hath spat upon the face of the Lord!

Whittier township, a dead woman says to ye future generations,

From this black place in a forgotten grave:

Ye are damned heathens in thy midst!

Ye reprobates!

Ye are not the chosen people!

Instead of worship, and disciplined prayer time,

Ye sit in the dumbing darkness and find Lucifer,

Dreaded star of the morning!

The Optic be damned!

PROLOGUE

POEM 130
# HOMER BRUNETT
# 1879–1912

You didn't think it would be easy?

Did you?

Life squirms incessantly,

As with the molting snake,

Turning and squeezing into mortal convolutions,

With myriad forgotten episodes

Of human triumph and tragedy,

Of endless drama in the slatted houses;

Life is constantly lurching and lunging, ever forward,

Under those silent indifferent clouds, up there!

But time is the ultimate mind master,

He knows where the switches to the stop gates are.

He knows when to open the field sluices awash!

We foolish human beings inevitably

Get taken by the rushing flood waters,

Get completely swept away by the undertow,

Helpless against the madding confluence,

Ending up as tears on the faces of the bereaved.

This is my final testament and statement!

That of an intelligent dead man!

# DIGESTED BY THE DUST

POEM 131

## JOHN MOORE
## 1843-1933

I was born with my lungs full of tarnation.

Leastways that was my mother's version of it.

I do not believe anyone who was ever born,

Came into this world kicking,

Leastways not like me;

I tumbled in, kicking like some drifting no account sodbuster,

Ready for the new plough, and the hedge maul.

I grew up in a working family;

My paw farmed our land with maw darning our lives together.

I grew up fast in this torrid sun, working and learning.

With sun-burned hands and forehead,

I scraped a living together, best I could,

And planted the seeds of a thousand children!

But with each passing shivering winter,

Even here in these sunny digs called Whittierville,

I hated the galloping return of the pale horse;

The dreaded infections of the lungs and nose;

Terrible suffering has taken place here, my friends,

Entire families were wiped out in a week,

Slain by a monster with no body!

Leastways that was my mother's version of it.

This old gravelly graveyard here was busy in 1918;

## THE VOICES FROM MT. OLIVE CEMETERY

Last stop for so many friends who died in a dark sick room,

Astonished, I might say, that it was their time to die;

I reckon Mt. Olive, in its greedier times of soft earth,

Has seen half a dozen funerals in a single day.

Leastways that's what I hear tell,

Coming from Artilissa Dorland Clark herself!

Those were scary times, and the years were dark.

I do not believe anyone who has ever died,

Left this world kicking,

Leastways, not like me... last thing I remember,

I reached up to the ceiling in my sick bed,

And cursed my damned lungs!

For once again, as if by intelligent design,

They were full of tarnation.

## DIGESTED BY THE DUST

POEM 132

# LENA LANE
# 1894–1912

Dying at 18 was my punishment from God.

"Bless me Heavenly Father, for I have sinned."

Johnny Barrow found the silk ribbon,

The only man man enough to look for it;

For I did not resist his insistent male charms,

That day in Turnbull, that rich awkward moment in time,

When two decided heartbeats and one determined hand,

Found the scented red ribbon,

Concealed most discretely upon my airy bosom.

Shame and sin indeed found us receptive that day;

He and me, staring awestruck at blue sky and white skin;

But I am fine with this legacy of private meetings,

And alas, private audacious touchings;

If only kindly Estella knew, poor sick soul;

Johnny really loved her; all the stars above admit that.

But Johnny wanted me, desired me with wanton civility,

Wanted me for the grand games we played in secret,

Touching games, grand groping games,

In the hidden lacey canyons of Turnbull.

If only kindly Estella knew, that poor homely thing;

Poor sick and disheveled girl!

Over there in your shriveled grave!

## THE VOICES FROM MT. OLIVE CEMETERY

I took your boy, Estella!

I took brown-eyed Johnny Barrow,

And branded him with my fiery mark!

## DIGESTED BY THE DUST

POEM 133
# EDWARDO BADIA
# 1856–1914

That low bred confidence man!

That snooking swindler who took me for a fool.

"Hey Gregg, you thief!

You owe me still, even as I rot here,

Regrettably ensconced inside this bursting old boneyard,

Final resting grounds of a thousand parted pilgrims,

No doubt suffering in claustrophobic hell,

Like this old besotted soul,

Decades and repeating weeks of years,

After Mister White planted me in this dusty earth,

Next to the famished broad oak over here,

A few yards from the stone crosses of the Luetweilers,

Buried and cushioned in the wrong grave,

Stuffed inside the tomb of a swindled corpse!

Sir, we shook hands on that deal!

I was to be transferred to Whittier Heights,

My new spacious home for these dusty old bones,

In exchange for the procurement of land there,

Burial land with pleasant vistas, green grass, and

"Eternally sweeping views of the Pacific,"

Fitting views indeed, for my sweet wife and loving mother;

And although my family was ceremoniously exhumed,

## THE VOICES FROM MT. OLIVE CEMETERY

And taxied there by a duo of horses and a trio of men,

Sir, you forgot me here, forlorn and alone,

And still in this detested grave!

How could you knowingly leave me here,

Separated and apart from my sweet wife,

And my loving mother?

Sir, I demand a refund!

## POEM 134
# MARY YELVINGTON
# 1876–1910

George Towne, now there was a man;

Handsome as the devil;

Strong as a bougainvillea vine.

And married to the redoubtable Fannie Towne,

Town shill, and occasional teetotaler of the dry brew!

Ol' Fannie was oblivious to the treasure she owned;

That incredible athlete!

That insufferable charmer!

At least after 3 o'clock, on most afternoons,

She never knew,

Or cared one iota really, where her man was!

Other than the little dramas concerning the Townes,

Life in Whittier, at the turn of the 20th Century,

Was boring, I must say.

Boring as a book with no danger!

Dangerous days never arrived for me,

Nor did I ever make the acquaintance of a dangerous man.

My life's journey indeed found intended joy,

Ecstatic joy in singing the hymns at church;

And it found surprised sadness as well,

In not surviving pneumonia at age 34.

And now, here I am, buried deep in the dark dirt,

Of shady Mt. Olive Cemetery.

But if only I had tried.

Tried to whistle, and nestle up to the big lug;

The day I saw him at Central Park,

Sitting on a bench with his prim coat and hat,

The incredibly dangerous George Towne!

DIGESTED BY THE DUST

POEM 135

# GLENN HERVEY
# 1880–1918

On the last day of my life,

I told God not to take me,

Not until some time past 3 p.m.,

My alone time for drinks, smokes

And other delicate divertissements.

I prayed from my deathbed for one last cigar,

And the required two hours to smoke it.

But God was not to be deterred that day!

In the age of men, I was a practicing "Man!"

Not to say I had the idle time for such a title.

I worked hard for my family;

Provided a good and bountiful life for them,

And when it was time to holler with the boys,

Well, by Fantods' Hand, I was there! And,

You could find me over to the big hotel on Saturdays,

Where secret recipes were made manifest,

With red carnations draped over white table cloths.

And beautiful ladies sat with men from the east.

There was much bustle to see from there,

From that open-air veranda out front,

Looking down Greenleaf Avenue through the trees!

I recall the endless movement of human forms,

## THE VOICES FROM MT. OLIVE CEMETERY

Scampering and scuttling like pigeons pecking for seed,

Way down there in the distance,

Through the darkened elders,

Keeping appointments, buying fruit,

And partaking, of course,

In other delicate divertissements.

Dying for me was easy.

I simply thought of my mother,

And then, the candle inside my mind,

Went out.

## DIGESTED BY THE DUST

**POEM 136**

# DAISY MAGILL
# 1889–1919

A person knows when she will die.

I knew it.

My uncle Harry knew it.

And my consumption knew it too.

My dying day was a sunny one, my friends.

As the July sun bathed my garden flowers outside,

I felt my life force slowly ebb away from me,

There, inside my lilac-filled bedroom on Comstock,

And I knew, all the hours of that dreaded day,

That I would soon be buried in my cozy coffin here,

In this weedy tract of Mt. Olive Cemetery,

Under these friendly walnut trees.

And while struggling to stay awake that last hour,

From my final sleep of death,

I thought back in painful anguish,

Back to my youthful carefree days,

When I was seventeen,

And my long auburn hair was in braids;

When my friends were all alive and happy,

And when life was good and free under the sun.

But Time took control of the reigns,

Of my coming days and years,

And more often than not,

Left me weeping for the past.

The past, when I had my time of incredible magic!

A single rapturous moment of utter bliss!

With him!

Roscoe Settle and me that day!

Meeting secretly at twilight time,

Embracing and kissing wildly,

Under these friendly walnut trees,

Here in weedy Mt. Olive Cemetery.

## POEM 137
## OSCAR D. COUCH
## 1885–1914

So your poet, Mr Hunter, here,

Has given me some writing space,

Strictly twenty five lines of epitaph,

For inclusion into this ponderous tome of his.

And despite being a dead man,

Going on over a hundred year now,

I have accepted his curious challenge herewith,

And offer up my final ode to human existence,

One in which the costumes of my very survival,

Were often altered and quickly changed,

Well before the tainted soup was ever served!

My obscure advice?

Be careful of bashful friends.

Shhh! Keep your voice low around the quiet ones.

Shhh! Never confide to the shy ones your secret plans.

Roscoe was my good friend, I must confess.

He was as shy a boy I had ever known.

Good at football, and shooting arrows with a bow.

And he was an expert with trees and shrubbery.

But if you want me to comment about his sex life,

Mister Hunter! Mister Poet Man!

Well, you can just forget it!

Roscoe was misunderstood! That I know.

And his sudden death was most tragic to me.

But leave me out of it, Mister Stark Hunter!

Mister Poet Man with the license!

## POEM 138
# CYRUS NEFF
# 1842-1914

You will never find me and the missus,

Not back here amongst the roots and the scrubs!

We are among the forgotten dead of Mt. Olive Cemetery.

Our graves have disappeared, completely

Eaten away by time and rain and wind.

I bought these cheap graves in a potters field, my friends.

Mt. Olive is nothing more than a cheap graveyard,

Just a donated acre of Quaker farm land,

Given over to the community to bury the poor,

And the early dead; those poor pioneering souls,

Succumbing slowly to the poisons of diphtheria in 1887.

But we survivors are snoring away still, out here,

Behind this dense crowd of whispering walnut trees,

Which bend a little in the September wind,

And dutifully guard the grave of Greek George, over there.

Truth be known, me and the missus loved it here in Whittier.

We had a nice house on dusty Penn Street,

Over by the spreading Hybrid tree,

And enjoyed a brace of decades under the California sun,

Living, working, and then dying.

My friends, you are all invited to our graves,

The missus and me, well, you won't find us here.

## THE VOICES FROM MT. OLIVE CEMETERY

For we are now one with the roots and the scrubs!

But you are invited to come by, sit a spell,

And listen with us, the missus and me,

To the whispering voices of the walnut trees.

DIGESTED BY THE DUST

POEM 139
# IVIE TWOMBLEY
# 1884–1913

Lottie Gordon and me were always together.

Joined at the hip, most folks would say;

You never met two ladies quite like us.

If you had known Lottie and Ivie,

The two of us at age 21,

If you had gotten to know us for our real selves;

Wild bachelorettes in french garters,

Roaming the Quaker streets and alleys,

Of Greenleaf, Philadelphia and Bailey,

Seeking out young mammon, and innocent kisses,

As we did quite regularly in 1905,

Why, you would have summoned our parents!

And the Elders of the Friends Church to boot!

Lottie and me were soulful sisters,

And best friends, especially in the snaring arts,

Trapping both wild men and civilized beasts alike!

It didn't seem to matter one way or the other really,

Not after what happened to Roscoe.

We all knew someone murdered him.

As we both knew everyone hated him.

My Lottie, she never recovered from losing that man.

It seared my soul to see that girl so broken-hearted. ...

## THE VOICES FROM MT. OLIVE CEMETERY

I think of her all the time, even now in death.

She's buried across Citrus Road in Clark Cemetery,

Over there by the old toppled stones,

And the high, giraffe-like, desert palms...

...The earth moves, my friends.

It moves without ceasing, without slowing,

We dead people can feel it rumble and grind and twist,

Rumble like an old machine in winter...

I met my demise at age 29.

I died like Lottie, drowning helplessly,

Without being in the water.

And that was that.

## POEM 140
# KENNETH STANDISH
# 1912-1919

We lived on Newlin Street in a gray house,

Across from the Catholic church, St. Mary's.

I loved going to the Mass every morning,

Which I did daily with my shirt tucked in.

Until my kidney sickness stopped me.

I would have been a altar boy,

Had I lived longer.

But I hated Catholic school with that nun!

She was mean to me.

One time, I had my shirttail out in class,

And got a loud scolding from Sister Evangela.

I was embarrassed and turned red, and the kids laughed.

But I got over it fast enough.

Still, I loved all the gospel stories we heard,

And recess time with the fellas;

Wish I could go to school again.

Wish I could see my friends at the wall.

We all played "four-square" there during recess.

Wish I could live again, and play ball.

Wish I could see mom and pop in the kitchen again,

As they were, young and hard-working,

And as always telling me to wash my hands and eat.

## THE VOICES FROM MT. OLIVE CEMETERY

I can still hear their same familiar voices,

Inside our old gray house on Newlin Street.

The front door, it seemed, was always open.

But now, well, there is no door where I am.

This graveyard is strange at night.

I hear footsteps on the paths above me, and

I wonder who is up there, when I hear them.

# DIGESTED BY THE DUST

POEM 141

## LAURAH MAYBELLE RICKBORN
## 1907–1935

Life was such a excruciating bother.

I'm happy the long drama is finished now.

My childhood consisted mostly of chores and lessons,

While my teenage years were devoted to daydreams,

Dancing, and the work I did ceaselessly,

On my parents' modest farm on Painter Avenue.

Indeed, I acquired the dogmatic idea early in life,

That chickens are undoubtedly the filthiest creatures,

Ever created by our very creative creator.

So it was with a strange dose of personal joy,

Whenever I accosted one of our hapless chickens by its neck,

For the celebrated purpose of a quick slaughter.

Then, with speedy relish, I'd chop its beady head off;

Finally, with determined aplomb, I defeathered the thing,

As it death-spasmed still on my bloody lap.

Such are the memories I choose to remember,

As my final pathetic epitaph,

Of a life I found ultimately annoying and frustrating;

Of having to put up with arrogant selfish men,

Who smelled of cigars, whiskey and sweaty talcum;

And who desired more than a quick dance under the stars, indeed!

Of having to endure obtuse women with no life at all, except drudgery;

Simple-minded women who worked like willing slaves,

For their blow hard men-keepers; Blecch!

I wanted no part of that, thank you.

Like I said, I'm happy the drama is finished.

Happy, deliriously so, that

My daily encounters with conceited boorish men,

Are, at last, at an end!

Brava I say, to all women who fly freely!

Fly! Fly! Resist men! Fly!

# DIGESTED BY THE DUST

**POEM 142**
# JOHN B. JACKSON
# 1880–1911

Norma knew.

Norma, my erstwhile friend of a thousand hunts;

Only she knew the feel of my beading thumb,

As we sought out promising locales, and

Our clever quarry, from points near and far.

From the salty marshes by the Pio Pico adobe,

To the broad summit of Sycamore Canyon,

We left tracks only the night 'coons could find.

So, did we learn anything in life, me and Norma?

I once spied a tern furrowing in a breach.

Norma was ready and loaded for the kill,

As I drew a long bead,

Held my breath, and pulled the trigger.

She, my Winchester 1895, lever-action,

Reduced that tern to feathers in an instant of smoke,

With white pillow plumage in complete upheaval,

Flying all about, and interspersed asunder!

That single memory was on my mind,

Before slipping eternally through the veil.

I remember closing my eyes, and there she was!

Appearing before me as a haunting ghost,

As she was, on the day she saw me kill the tern,

## THE VOICES FROM MT. OLIVE CEMETERY

My disappointed mother, telling me I was cruel,

Cruel and heartless and mean,

For destroying "God's creature."

So, it was on that same day I put Norma away,

Lock, stock and barrel; stowed in silence,

Under the rafters of my humble bed;

I said a final goodbye and adios amiga,

To my once ballistic sweetheart,

And the love of my wild, youthful days.

Never again did I kill any living creature,

And found an inner wisdom I could never explain.

But, truth be known,

I wish I had Norma now.

Here in this dark cold grave.

I miss the tender touch of her cold trigger.

The gentle pull of her icy hammer.

And mostly, I miss the intoxicating power,

Of her fiery, exploding steel.

For together we traversed the canyons of Turnbull,

And the rolling vernal pastures of Workman Mill,

Tasting many a delicious quarry.

It's true, my friends,

Norma knew.

Only she knew the feel of my beading thumb.

## POEM 143

# BESSIE M. GOOD
# 1890–1913

By the time I was 21 years along,

I had given birth to two girls,

Nadine and Ruth, my precious babies.

Both had eyes of tea green,

With perfect fragrant cheeks,

Softly redolent of sweet-smelling spice-

That special baby smell- Heaven's spice,

And both were loved completely,

By a strong soulful love,

Immensely deep and earth-real;

Only women who have dutifully dropped

Their blessed ten pound bundle,

Upon this love-lonely, cursed world,

Can attest to this compelling love,

This gripping, primordial bonding,

This indescribable link to the hand of God!

And so, it is to God I ask this question- Why?

Why did you take Nadine from me?

My sweet baby! Why?

I cried shrieking in hysterical circles;

My husband Henry sat motionless

And staring downward, inert.

## THE VOICES FROM MT. OLIVE CEMETERY

For many days and weeks we mourned,

Never really getting over it;

How does one recover from the death of a child? How?

Then God answered our prayers with sweet Ruth!

Adorable, innocent beautiful Ruth!

For two wonderful years we were together,

Then, unexpectedly, Death took my sweet Ruth...

Why God?

Why did you take Ruth from me?

My sweet baby! Why?

I cried shrieking in hysterical circles!

Here in my dusty forgotten grave,

At shady Mt Olive Cemetery,

The deep pain of such heartbreaking episodes,

Which killed me slowly by age 23,

Has long ebbed away from me.

And now, no one remembers or cares, about

What happened to me and my girls,

Many shaded years ago.

And finally, my epitaph:

Life has always had its tragedies,

At least that's what all my teachers said.

My advice?

Get right with God.

POEM 144
# CLINTON LYNCH
# 1862–1912

It took a long time for me to die.

Five long years; from the moment

Doctor Barmore told me my heart was bad,

Until the day I was on my deathbed,

Staring listlessly through my envious window,

At a world that was alive with people living,

A truly strange and wonderful world, that

Was presently passing before me,

Like a final grand parade in time,

With all my old friends, dead now,

Waving from carriages festooned in gladioli.

In the end, I had no living friends. Instead,

I had my elderly mother tend to me,

With stern patience, and kind forbearance.

At my funeral, here at Mt. Olive,186

Eleven people attended my final rites,

Performed ably by the coughing Pastor Hadley.

My final epitaph is nothing grand or profound;

It is simply a simple farewell,

From a simple man,

Who lived a simple life.

And it is okay if no one remembers me.

POEM 145
# CLEMENTINE LYON
# 1917–1918

Little does anyone remember,

That when the wee little birth door opens,

And the first light blindingly shines through,

Death is standing there,

Laughing,

With his sticky net swishing to catch you.

But tiny me, how lucky I was.

I survived the birth plunge;

I made it through, squirmingly,

To this strange turning green world,

This larger extending net,

Made of twine from the beard of past days,

Where destined time holds sway,

Where Death continues to hunt young meat.

My worldly stay was short and sad.

And I am mindful that I never had friends,

Or that I ever walked under a tree.

# DIGESTED BY THE DUST

POEM 146

# GEORGE FULWIDER
# 1837–1918

My beating-heart age,

Reached the half century mark,

When I and my "better second,"

Found hopeful roots,

And an oleander trellis,

On burgeoning Philadelphia street,

Here in this Quaker colony,

Of a thousand trees.

Our small wooded house was,

Most unfortunately,

Within earshot of the stately Union High School,

And its noisy ragamuffin minions,

And inescapably contiguous,

With the bustling tentacled trolley tracks;

Up and down they groaned,

With their loud clanging,

Every day and night the house shook,

As they rumbled on by,

Those modern moving monsters,

With steely grinding wheels,

Made ever alive by,

Those drat hanging wires,

Of killing electricity;

The doom of progress was upon us!

Oh, for the olden days!

The simpler times!

When life was for the strong and the smart,

Not like it was, when I,

Gasping for air in 1918,

Said goodbye to this silly modern world,

This long life,

This unending waiting game.

Now my restless stifled ghost,

Haunts the dark grounds here,

Roaming o'er the stones and the shadows,

At midnight when the wind dies,

Seeking still, a moment of hopeful silence, no,

An entire afterlife,

Of sweet heavenly golden silence,

Away from those modern moving steely monsters,

Those groaning grinding interlopers,

Of killing electricity;

The doom of progress is upon you!

POEM 147

# WALTER B. CANFIELD
# 1872–1914

It is in my best interest indeed,

Now that my name is about to be called,

To come forth to the White Throne,

To make confession, and to be judged,

For my legion of sins and trespasses,

Committed in no small part, as

The irresistible charms of one Lutie Sayles,

Precluded any semblance of forthright fidelity.

For she was the devil's mate, this I knew,

As time and time again,

She flirtingly tapped my arm with a coy smile,

As I passed the collection plate to her at Sunday services,

Young and beautiful and available Lutie Sayles,

Seated in her usual polished corner pew,

With wild flowers set in her brown curls,

While I, dressed in clean suit and tailored tie,

Privately entertained inside my mincing mind,

Not thoughts of Job or Enoch,

But secret visions of Lutie and me,

Ensconced together on a green terrace,

Surrendering to the elements of stardust, wind,

And wet puckered lips,

Ultimately finding sinful solitude,

Under a dying cedar tree,

On wind-swept Rideout Ranch.

Oh, be not alarmed at these fantasies,

Of a man now dead for a century,

For church was truly boring,

And I, a man and nothing else,

Found the winsome Lutie Sayles

In my every waking thought.

Then it happened, as if by serendipity,

I saw Lutie Sayles on the side of Workman Mill Road,

That drowsy sleepy day,

When Providence appeared as a descending swan,

And with subtle all encompassing power,

Parted Lutie's Red Sea,

For my charging manly chariot!

### DIGESTED BY THE DUST

POEM 148

# MARIA FLORES
# 1878–1923

Si, he was muy macho!
I was the last to see him.
Before Senor White sealed his body for eternity,
Inside the cheapest casket I had ever seen!
And I was working there, for White-Emerson,
From the time I was 16,
Combing the dead's hair, and mixing make-up.
Señora White, she put the make-up on their faces,
And I stood back by the door and watched.
At first, it was two or three bodies a week,
Mostly white folk, stiff and cold as ice;
They were Whittier people I did not know;
Older folk with life's road behind them,
And young childer, brought in by wailing parents,
Dead from sickness and accident.
I prayed for these poor people because they were sad.
Later, the visits of the ever-marching dead,
Became a more common event,
Every day he, Señor White, brought the dead in,
Every day I combed their hair.
This I did until I myself died in 1923,
Giving birth to my still-born son.

Then it was my turn for Señora White,

To apply my face with fake life;

Her creams, rinses and perfumes, magically,

Made me appear as alive as I was.

But oh, I wish now to trick fake death,

And live again,

Be there again,

Down in the dark embalming room,

There at White Emerson, with him.

Si, he was muy macho!

And yes, I was the girl to love Roscoe last!

Me, a nobody Mexican with little money.

Shh, let us whisper now.

Let us be quiet and honest;

I was the last one to coddle him there,

The last to stroke his lifeless bill,

My eagle of a man!

There in the still darkness,

He, the most handsome boy,

My eyes had ever seen!

Dead and lifeless there,

In my secret embrace!

Dead in my controlling grasp!

I combed his locks for two hours,

And prayed, yes, I prayed,

## DIGESTED BY THE DUST

For his departed soul, and body too,

For, let it be known to all,

For it no longer matters at all,

I was the last girl to have him.

Muy Macho!

POEM 149
# FRANK OSGOOD
# 1870–1919

I was the great wanderlust of Whittier!

From 1890 until my last days,

I followed my nose,

And other body appendages,

To distant earthly destinations,

Both sensational and disgusting,

From the calm tranquility of a secure home,

To the chaos and uncertainty,

Of traveling with heavy bags, aching feet,

And certain fears, I, nevertheless,

Decided to break out and seek other lands,

Other people, and other vistas.

Sickness did awfully afflict me many times,

As I lay retching inside many a tent,

But always I was learning, and thriving.

To far-away Rome I traipsed,

To Paris, Venice and London too.

From the streets of Madrid to

The far-away shores of the Mediterranean,

Where The Christ founded a mighty religion,

I ventured and saw, and tasted!

I hunted on safari in Eastern Africa and

## DIGESTED BY THE DUST

Shot a gazelle from a standing position.

In beautiful South America and Asia,

My restless feet found another universe,

Of unworldly sights and strange rituals.

My friends!

It was amazing indeed to drink it all in,

Like a cool fruit drink from Rio.

But my thirst for wandering was never slaked.

And then it ended,

Like the quick waking from a dream,

When I died at home of a measly fever.

Most ironic indeed.

And so, as for my epitaph, This is it:

"'Tis a heap of profit to travel."

POEM 150
## JOHN DOE
## BURIED 1913 (ESTIMATED AGE 35)

When Death opened its revolving door,

And pulled my screaming soul in,

I found out the truth.

So, here it is fellow citizens of Whittier town,

Both known and unknown,

From John Doe,

Stabbed to death one moonless night,

Over a poker game gone wrong,

That nameless rotting corpse

You found floating that long-ago day,

In the deep river by Pio Pico.

I found out

There is no ending.

The story never ceases to be.

Time and your soul continue on.

Here, where I am now,

On this side of the grave,

The book that you are reading,

Does not have a final page.

The song that you are hearing,

Does not stop playing.

The journey that you are taking,

Will never reach its ultimate destination.

If you throw a stone into the well,

It will never hit bottom.

I found out

This is the way of all striving flesh,

When your number is solemnly called... ...

Timeless eternity..........

Permit me now to say a definitive goodbye,

On behalf of all these forlorn dead,

Who now lie reposed as bones and dust,

Interred snugly and deeply,

Very deeply,

Under these lapping walnut trees,

Here in old Mt. Olive Cemetery.

Does anyone remember us?

Remember our names and addresses?

Our appearances and voices?

Of course not.

Sleep everyone.

Sleep deeply

Very deeply, and dream

Of being remembered again.

# EPILOGUE

## THE POET'S REMEMBRANCES OF HIS FIRST VISIT
## INSIDE CLARK CEMETERY - MAY, 1964

A week before Memorial Day weekend they came - A crew of about fifteen men wearing silver hard hats and blue shirts and driving six big red trash trucks. With shovels and rakes and pitch forks and pruning shears and sunburned faces they came, to rescue the forgotten dead of Clark Cemetery. When I walked by on a Monday toward the end of May, they were inside both sections of the cemetery frantically clearing up the mountain of weeds and debris, and pruning back all the dense trees and restoring the dozens of toppled tombstones on their rightful pedestals.

By my count, it took a full five days for this small army of city workers to finish the job, and when it was done, I swear I could hear a thousand silent voices screaming their "Thank You's" through the western and eastern gates. As I gazed at all those naked tombstones and the landscape that was now manicured, I was intensely impressed with the view; for the condemned graveyard now had a strange magnificent beauty about it. It was as if I had gone back in time to the turn of the century when Clark Cemetery was an integral part of the community, open and accessible; a colorful sacred garden where surviving relatives could come in their horse-drawn carriages to pay their respects, leave home-grown bouquets and perhaps find psychological solace over their devastating loss.

When Memorial Day weekend arrived I was extremely relieved, for it meant three days off from school, and it was also a sure sign that the end of the school year was nigh. I had plans to spend that Saturday afternoon listening to the Dodger game, as usual, and playing catch with my friend on the front dicondra lawn. However, when my father and I drove by the cemetery that morning, I noticed with tremendous interest that the western and eastern gates were unlocked and wide open. And so I decided to alter those plans. My request to my father was brief and to the point. "Dad, the graveyard is open. Can we go inside today?" His reply came in the form of an affirmative nod; simple with no hesitation.

It was late morning when my father and I silently walked over to the western gate on Citrus Avenue on that sunny Memorial Day in 1964, and when I entered into this immaculately clean world of the dead for the first time, I was in awe of the place. There was an unmistakable aura of subdued energy, and I felt a flood of sadness dripping from all those trees. I vividly recall the hairs on my arms stood erect, and I felt goose bumps all over my skin. It was a feeling I had not experienced before... and I loved it.

We slowly strolled together without a word being said, and I recollect taking my time, reading every name on each tombstone that we passed, and I made a point in looking at the year of their demise. And as I looked intensely upon each name, I memorized many of them, and I thought about many things. I silently wondered where each dead person was born, and where each was when their heart stopped beating. And I wondered what each person's last word was, and on what day their eyes closed for the last time. And I thought about what each looked like when they were my age; their hair color and eye color and how tall, and how many gallons of tears each shed in the course of their lifetime.

I can still remember some of their last names; names that were etched carefully and largely in thick ponderous stone, reminding me of those big headlines I had seen on the front page of the LA Times when Kennedy was shot; strange, unusual names like Hunnicutt, Bemix, Milhous, Rasmussen, Skumfeldt, Fulwider. I also noticed numerous, old cracked graves of husbands and wives, now sleeping together in their eternal beds beneath the hard sod; names I will never forget - Donald and Gertrude Langstaff who passed away in 1926 and in 1939, and Henry and Eva Metcalf with the death dates of 1917 and 1927 on their large broad tombstone, and Cyrus and Hester Neff who were located in the farthest reaches of the cemetery, way in the back corner right next to Mrs. Tyrone's backyard fence, nestled by two tall desert palm trees; graves that only just a short week before had been forgotten and virtually swallowed up by a mountain of dead weeds. And I silently fantasized about their long ago funerals off in this forgotten, obscure corner of the graveyard which took place in 1914 for Cyrus and 1917 for Hester. Who grieved for these people? And where are these mourners now? And if they're dead now, who in turn mourned for them? I remember also speculating how the Metcalfs appeared on their wedding day, perhaps a hundred years ago, and the beaming smiles on their young faces that day, and I wondered if their wedding rings were there...under the ground...in the cold blackness...still adorning skeletal hands that once held and caressed each other on lazy summer afternoons.

One section of the cemetery, also located far in the back, was exclusively for infants. There must've been twenty, perhaps thirty babies buried there, all with no first names; just last names and the distant dates of their still births inscribed crudely by hand. There was no dirt here, just full-length slabs of cracked concrete - the cheapest gravestone money could barely buy.

Directly in the middle of this graveyard was an old walnut tree that apparently broke apart when it first started growing back in the 1880's, and then later on, two separate trees began to grow independent of each other; one growing to the left toward Broadway street, and the other growing to the right toward the houses on the other side of the north barbed wire fence. Located at the base of this strange, "two-headed" tree was another husband and wife grave; only this grave was not the typical huge monument with the last name boldly carved on the crest. But instead, this marker was a simple white cross made of alabaster, and on it I noticed the names Frederick G. Waddell, 1893-1919 and Kathrene Mary Waddell, 1899-1921. And I recall as I stood there in the mid-day sun with my father close by smoking his second Pall Mall cigarette of the walk, I let my imagination go, and I tried to visualize in my rather morbid mind what these two dead people looked like, and what could have possibly killed both of them off so early in their young lives. Using my questionable arithmetic skills, I calculated that Frederick was only 26 when he died, and his wife Kathrene was but 22 years of age when she breathed her last, and it didn't make sense to me. Nor did all those pauper graves for all those nameless infants who never tasted life, even for a minute. And I angrily asked myself: "What's the point? Why is there death in life?" Then I turned around and asked my father: "Why do we have to die?" At first he seemed a bit dumbfounded by my question, but soon understood the context and responded quietly, for my father was a quintessentially quiet man with short logical answers to all my questions. "People get old," he said. "They get sick. The body breaks down after a while. The heart stops beating. The lungs stop breathing." Then I remember he said: "These two here...died young. They probably caught a disease...maybe the flu. People used to die from that back when I was a kid."

"Geez, I like getting the flu," I professed with strong honesty. "I can stay home from school and watch TV all day."

"Times have changed," my father mused. "People died younger back then, and women often died just giving birth. I suppose we're lucky to be alive these days. Doctors know more."

"Yeah, I guess so."

And then I spotted the Lutweiler gravestone; probably the largest and saddest monument in all of Clark Cemetery. It was at least eight feet high and about six feet wide, made of gray polished marble and painstakingly decorated with dozens of lilies. The plot itself was a perfect square; an area as big as the front parlor room of my Hoover street house, lined on all four sides with narrow concrete slabs resembling roadside curbs, no more than a foot high and a foot across, and I vividly recall the slabs were cracked and no longer connected together because of the shifting of the land throughout the decades. Inside this large plot of rocky, hardened dirt contained five graves: Jacob, 1865-1948; Fannie, 1879-1936; and their three small children: Lena, 1901-1904; Norma May, 1901-1902 and Lester, 1903-1905. As I stood there taking in this gravesite of an entire family, I could honestly feel the pain and heartbreak of twenty thousand sunsets ago inside that small plot of dead land, feel the inundation of tears welling up from under the ground and soaking my feet, and I turned and walked away, not wanting to drown in this bubbling lake of forgotten grief and madness.

By the time the sun was at its highest point, I could tell my father was growing restless with our stroll through eternity that had by now taken up about ninety minutes.

"Getting ready for lunch?" he asked, stomping out his third cigarette on the hard dead ground.

"I'm ready."

# ABOUT THE AUTHOR

Born in Whittier, California in 1952, Stark Hunter was an English teacher for 38 years before retiring from the classroom in 2017. He has also written and published 7 other books, which are available on Amazon.com and Barnes & Noble.com: *In A Gadda Da Vida*, published in 2002, *Carnivorous Avenues*, a poetry volume published in 2004, *Flies*, a short novel published in 2005, *Private Diaries*, a satire published in 2006, *Voices From Clark Cemetery*, a poetry volume published in 2013, *Cocktails For the Soul*, a poetry anthology published in 2013, and *Voices From Mt. Olive Cemetery*, a poetry volume published in 2018.

Mr. Hunter is also a published photographer, having one of his photographs included in the book, *Photography Vibes, Best of Edition* in 2008.

Fourteen of Mr. Hunter's poems from *Voices From Clark Cemetery* were adapted and set to music by Dr. George Mabry, composer and former conductor of the Nashville Symphony Chorus, for his work, *Voices*, a musical drama which was performed at Austin Peay State University in Clarksville, Tennessee in 2015.

Mr. Hunter's poetry works can be perused at Poetrysoup.com, and his photography is on display at JPGMag. Com. Mr. Hunter's blog site is Stark Hunter's Mind Tavern@wordpress.com.

Mr. Hunter is married with two daughters, a granddaughter, and resides in Chino Hills, California.

www.ingramcontent.com/pod-product-compliance
Lightning Source LLC
LaVergne TN
LVHW041608070426
835507LV00008B/172